The ABC's of Classroom Management

An A–Z sampler for designing your learning community

by Pamela A. Kramer
and Kappa Delta Pi

Kappa Delta Pi,
International Honor Society
in Education

Indianapolis, Indiana

Kappa Delta Pi, International Honor Society in Education
3707 Woodview Trace, Indianapolis, Indiana 46268-1158

Printed in the United States of America

05 06 07 08 09 5 4 3 2 1

ISBN 0-912099-43-7

Direct all inquiries to the Director of Publications, Kappa Delta Pi, 3707
Woodview Trace, Indianapolis, IN 46268-1158.

Executive Director   Assistant Editor
Michael P. Wolfe   *Helen McCarthy*

Director of Publications   Design and Layout
Kathie-Jo Arnoff   *Chuck Jarrell, Cindy Kelley*

Series Editor   Cartoonist
Karen L. Allen   *Bill Allen*

Order copies through Kappa Delta Pi's International Headquarters at
800-284-3167 or the KDP Online Store at *www.kdp.org*. Quantity dis-
counts available for more than 20 copies. Use Store Order Code 536.

Library of Congress Cataloging-in-Publication Data
Kramer, Pamela A., 1956-
 The ABC's of classroom management : an A-Z sampler for designing your learning com-
munity /
by Pamela A. Kramer and Kappa Delta Pi
   p. cm.
 Includes bibliographical references.
 ISBN 0-912099-43-7
 1. Classroom management--Handbooks, manuals, etc. I. Kappa Delta Pi (Honor Society) II.
Title
 LB3013.K73 2005
 317.102'4--dc22
                                                              2005018967

About the Author

Bill Miller

- **Pamela A. Kramer** is a Professor of Education and Assistant to the
  Chair in the Department of Early Childhood and Elementary Education
  at East Stroudsburg University of Pennsylvania. Her array of educational
  expertise includes 18 years in teacher education, nine years of teaching
  at the elementary level, and coordinating programs with professional
  development schools. She currently instructs on principles and practices
  of teaching, psychology of elementary school children, and elementary
  science methods.

  Dr. Kramer earned her doctorate at Lehigh University in Bethlehem,
  Pennsylvania. She is also the Chapter Counselor of the Gamma Xi
  Chapter of Kappa Delta Pi.

Acknowledgments

Kappa Delta Pi Publications would like to thank the following
individuals who shared their expertise in producing this book.

Reviewers
Doug Brown
Karen Dunham
Monique Gallet
Kathryn Heaston
Jasmine Lind
Lisa Magnelli
Amy Troyer
Jessica Watkins
Kim Williams

Contributors
Jennifer Cole
Erika Lee
Sarah Wolfe

Table of Contents

Z

Sidebars

Extras

About This Book

Some things just aren't as simple as ABC—and classroom management is one of those. Most teachers, whether they have two days or 20 years of teaching experience, would say that managing a classroom is one of the most challenging aspects of teaching. Learning how to manage a group of students is not easy. Though experience hones skills, each group of students is unique and may respond differently to strategies that worked well previously. For this reason, teachers must acquire a broad repertoire of strategies to draw upon when developing classroom expectations and managing student behaviors.

Classroom management is an ongoing learning process. It is not mastered in a single course, one year of teaching, or from reading this book. From basic concepts to specific ideas, however, this book provides solid information from experienced teachers to put you in control of your classroom. Through the quick-search format of this book, busy teachers can find practical tips and effective strategies for handling common classroom problems from the first day of school and throughout the year.

As you explore *The ABC's of Classroom Management,* watch for these icons—they flag important information:

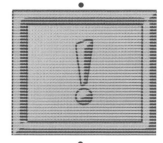

Pick up a quick tip about managing your classroom.

Get advice from experienced teachers.

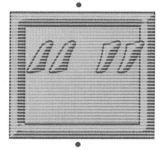

Read the inspirational words of professionals.

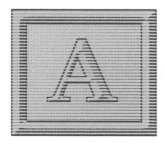

Anticipate

Anticipate anything. By anticipating potential questions, interruptions, and problems, you can better prepare for and lessen those unexpected incidents. One teacher, for instance, anticipated the oft-asked question "May I get a drink of water?" and had the children keep water bottles on their desks. Also see **Preventative Measures.**

Assume Nothing

False assumptions generate management challenges; they presume that students will understand because it is evident to the teacher. Watch what you assume. For example, don't take for granted that telling students to use "inside voices" will result in them conversing in near whispers. What if yelling is the norm at their household? Assumptions and vague expectations poke loopholes in any classroom-management plan. Don't "Swiss cheese" your plan—get classroom management off to a great start by specifically spelling out your expectations from the first day.

- Have students repeat your directions so that you know they understand.
- Give examples of expected behaviors.
- Model expected behaviors.
- Role-play appropriate behavior for and with students.
- Act out proper as well as obviously inappropriate conduct, and then have students reflect on the different scenarios.
- Repeat role-playing when incidents occur.
- Create a chart delineating responsibilities of the teacher and students (see example).
- Remind students of expectations throughout the year.

Teacher	Students
Create a safe learning environment.	Come to school on time.
Treat each student as an individual.	Come prepared to learn.
Facilitate learning.	Treat others with respect.
Provide frequent feedback.	Complete all assigned work.
Come prepared to teach.	Have a positive attitude.

Attendance

Take attendance and lunch count effortlessly using index and pocket cards—like those placed in library books to hold return-date cards. With these cards, lunch count and attendance become part of the students' morning routine. Select a pocket card for each student and place the cards in alphabetical order on a board or wall. Below the cards, hang two or three pockets—depending on the school's counting system—for color-coded index cards that signify school lunch, sack lunch, and milk only. A pocket without a card indicates that child is absent. This process, therefore, becomes part of each student's morning routine that includes putting away outerwear, choosing the appropriate card, and placing it in his or her corresponding name pocket.

Awards

See **Rewarding Positive Behavior.**

Be Human

Let students know you as a person. Being "human" is essential to establishing a healthy classroom community. Share information about your family, hobbies, and interests to let students know that you have a life outside of the classroom. Children often think teachers live in their classrooms! Decide what information is reasonable to share, taking care to maintain a professional distance. Students should not know intimate details of your life. See **Friends Frenzy.**

Behavior Management

Classroom and behavior management go hand-in-hand for a well-run classroom. Procedures and expectations set the stage for managing the classroom and student behaviors. Once the stage is set, teachers must develop rapport with students to affect student behavior and nurture learning. You can establish positive relationships with students by acting on five essential teacher behaviors, according to educator and *Cooperative Discipline* (1990 and 1996) author Linda Albert. These behaviors are: **acceptance, attention, appreciation, affirmation**, and **affection.** Teachers must go beyond simply accepting students. They must provide them with **attention**; show **appreciation** for them; **affirm** their desirable traits; and show them unconditional **affection,** kindness, and caring. For books by Albert, see **References** in **Extras.**

As part of their behavior-management program, some teachers reward positive student behaviors. For additional information about rewards, see **Rewarding Positive Behavior.**

Bibliotherapy

Using literature for therapeutic purposes is called bibliotherapy. Bibliotherapy is considered most helpful when identification, catharsis, and insight occur. Whether they read individually or in groups, when students read books that address problems they are experiencing, they can identify with characters and events to make emotional connections. Through guided discussion, students then can experience catharsis and gain possible resolutions to their dilemmas. Get your bibliotherapy library started with the list of books suggested here. They are grouped by topic and appropriate age levels.

Bibliotherapy list
Bullying

The Bad News Bully, Marcia Leonard (4–8)

The Bully Free Classroom: Over 100 Tips and Strategies for Teachers K–8, Allan L. Beane

Bully, Judith Caseley (4–8)

Bullies Are a Pain in the Brain, Trevor Romain (9–12)

How to Handle Bullies, Teasers and Other Meanies: A Book That Takes the Nuisance Out of Name Calling and Other Nonsense, Kate Cohen-Posey (9–12)

Jake Drake, Bully Buster, Andrew Clements (7–10)

My Secret Bully, Trudy Ludwig (9–12)

Nobody Knew What to Do: A Story about Bullying, Becky Ray McCain and Todd Leonardo (primary/intermediate grades)

Stick Up for Yourself: Every Kid's Guide to Personal Power and Positive Self-Esteem, Gershen Kaufman, Lev Raphael, and Pamela Espeland (9–12)

Loss of Grandparents, Parents, or Other Adults

Ages 4–8

After the Funeral, Jane Loretta Winsch and Pamela T. Keating

An Angel in the Sky, Coryn Gizcki-Lipson and Carlie Gizcki

Do Not Be Sad—A Chronicle of Healing, Chris Jarrin

The Fall of Freddie the Leaf, Leo Buscaglia

The Goodbye Boat, Mary Joslin and Claire S. Little

John Brown, Rose and the Midnight Cat, Jenny Wagner

My Grandma Died: A Child's Story About Grief and Loss, Lory Britain and Carol Deach

Sophie, Mem Fox

The Very Best of Friends, Margaret Wild

Where Is Grandpa? T. A. Barron

Why Did Grandpa Die? A Book about Death, Barbara Shook Hazen

Wilfrid Gordon McDonald Partridge, Mem Fox

Ages 9–12

Coping with Death, Shasta Gaughen

"I Wish I Could Hold Your Hand": A Child's Guide to Grief and Loss, Pat Palmer and Dianne O'Quinn Burke

A Song for Cecilia Fantini, Cynthia Astor and Anthony Turpin

Tear Soup, Pat Schweibert and Chuck Deklyen

What on Earth Do You Do When Someone Dies? Trevor Romain and Elizabeth Verdick

When Someone Dies, Sharon Greenlee and Bill Drath

Teens

How It Feels When a Parent Dies, Jill Krementz

I Will Remember You: What to Do When Someone You Love Dies: A Guidebook through Grief for Teens, Laura Dower

Teenagers Face to Face with Bereavement, Karen Gravelle and Charles Haskins

Loss of Other Children (Friends, Siblings)

Bridge to Terabithia, Katherine Paterson

The Class in Room Forty-Four: When a Classmate Dies, Lynn B. Blackburn

My Brother Stealing Second, Jim Naughton

A Taste of Blackberries, Doris Buchanan Smith

Telling Christina Goodbye, Lurlene McDaniel

Time to Let Go, Lurlene McDaniel

Divorce
Ages 4–8
Always my Dad, Sharon Dennis Wyeth

Dad Has a New Girlfriend, What about Me? Vicky Aldrich

Dinosaurs Divorce, Laurene Krasny Brown and Marc Brown

I Don't Want to Talk about It, Jeanie Franz Ransom and Kathryn Kunz Finney

I Have Two Dads, Linnea Schulz and Susan Aitken

The Little Flower Girl, Linda Trace Brandon

Mama and Daddy Bear's Divorce, Cornelia Spelman and Kathy Parkinson

Ages 9–12
Can Anyone Fix My Broken Heart? June Thomas Crews

Dear Mr. Henshaw, Beverly Cleary

Divorce Happens to the Nicest Kids, Michael S. Prokop

Don't Fall Apart on Saturdays! The Children's Divorce-Survival Book, Adoph Moser and David Melton

Don't Make Me Smile, Barbara Park

Change
The Burnt Stick, Anthony Hill (young adult)

Changes, Anthony Browne (preschool)

My Hiroshima, Junko Morimoto (4–8)

Moving
Ages 4–8
Alexander, Who's Not (Do You Hear Me? I Mean It!) Going to Move, Judith Viorst

Hey, New Kid! Betsy Duffey and Ellen Thompson

I'm Not Moving, Mama, Nancy White Carlstrom

Ira Says Goodbye, Bernard Waber

Lucy's New House, Barbara Taylor Cork

Matthew Jackson Meets the Wall, Patricia Reilly Giff

My Name Is María Isabel, Alma Flor Ada

The Berenstain Bears' Moving Day, Jan and Stan Berenstain

What's the Recipe for Friends? Greg M. Williamson and Greg Abele

Ages 9–12

Amber Brown Is Not a Crayon, Paula Danziger

Long Shot, Timothy Tocher

The Moving Book: A Kid's Survival Guide, Gabriel Davis

Skellig, David Almond

Loss of a Pet

Ages 4–8

Barn Kitty, June Kirkpatrick

For Every Dog an Angel, Christine Davis

The Tenth Good Thing about Barney, Judith Viorst

When Your Pet Dies, Diane Pomerance

Bullying

Batsche and Knoff (1994, 166) described bullying as "a form of aggression in which one or more students physically and/or psychologically (and more recently, sexually) harass another student repeatedly over a period of time." Bullies desire power, are typically antisocial, and appear to gain satisfaction from the harassment of others. With as many as 15 percent of children being victimized by bullies (Center for the Advancement of Mental Health Practices in Schools 2005), bullying can be a tremendous challenge for students, parents, and teachers.

One of the best ways to address bullying is to take preventative measures. Begin the year with a No Tolerance Policy on bullying, clearly identifying to students what constitutes bullying. Learn your school's policies and procedures regarding harassment and follow those regulations implicitly. If your school doesn't have a policy, set specific classroom rules about and consequences for bullying, and carry them out immediately. Too often, teachers look the other way or view bullying as a rite of passage, but school violence is too serious of an issue to ignore.

Giving students opportunities to learn empathy and effective communication techniques can help prevent bullying. Simulation exercises promote empathy, as in the example, "Playing the bully." Also, encourage parents and students to limit exposure to violence and to structure time away from school, spending it under appropriate supervision.

Playing the bully

Have students act out a situation where one student is singled out and harassed by a few bullies. Encourage students to discuss how the victim feels. You also might have them talk about possible motives for the bullies' actions. In creating the simulation, choose a victim whose ridiculed characteristic can't be associated specifically with anyone in your class. Students are quick to make inferences.

- Victims of bullies need help with their behaviors as well. Teach them strategies for dealing with bullies and have them practice assertiveness through role-playing. Use special programs on character building, peer mediation, and bully prevention accessible through your school, stores, or on the Internet (see **Resources** in **Extras**). Additionally, you can tackle this difficult topic with stories that promote empathy or build confidence, preferably before a problem occurs. Read children's books about bullying to the class or make them available in your classroom library. Start with books suggested in the **Bibliotherapy list.**

What need does the student fulfill by bullying?

Every student behavior in some way is a form of basic need-fulfillment. According to William Glasser (1990), all people share the need for love (including attention), power (including success and achievement), freedom (independence and choice), and fun (including laughter). Fulfilling these needs is the basic motivator behind almost every human behavior or misbehavior. Drawing from this concept, teachers must provide positive substitutes for those misbehaviors students engage in to meet their needs with the purpose of correcting the situation. For example, if a child chronically interrupts the flow of class by cracking jokes, the teacher might allow the student to entertain classmates with a joke-of-the-day. Granting such an occasion would fulfill the child's need for fun, power, love, and freedom—and quite possibly, the classmates' needs as well.

– Jennifer Cole, 4th-Grade Teacher, Horizon
Christian School, Indianapolis, Indiana

Burnout

Hooks (in Preskill and Jacobvitz 2001, 174) referred to burnout as a "concomitant risk for those who aspire to create excitement in their classrooms." Burnout can happen subtly and too easily to caring teachers. Don't wait until you need a remedy to seek solutions. Establish a healthy balance of work and play to stay vital. Have a life outside the classroom, and don't become all-consumed with your job. Share your challenges and concerns with colleagues—it helps to vent.

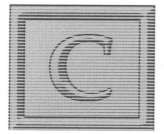

Capable, Connected, & Contributing

When students feel **capable** and **connected**, and they are **contributing** in the classroom, they acquire a sense of belonging. Feeling capable comes first, according to educator and *Cooperative Discipline* (1990 and 1996) author Linda Albert. A classroom atmosphere where mistakes are viewed as learn-ing opportunities encourages a sense of capability, as does boosting students' confidence and recognizing their achievements. Second, students must feel connected to their classmates and their teachers. Last, students must believe they are contributing to their worlds—the classroom and beyond. Community service and peer assistance present various opportunities through which students can contribute.

Choice

Student choice in the classroom: *choose* it, or not. Giving options to students may not yield the easiest or quickest way to approach a task, plan a lesson, or solve a problem, but it does successfully motivate students. It's successful because curriculum built on the interests and questions of the students, as well as their prior knowledge, cultivates a natural flow to lessons and engages students. The more engaged students are in their learning, the less often management issues arise.

Choices stimulate creativity and generate opportunities. At any grade level, allowing student choice acknowledges various learning styles and intelligences within the classroom. Presenting options for successful completion of an assignment—such as summarizing a book by drawing, writing, singing, or talking—demonstrates that learning and achievement can and do occur through one's natural talents.

With thousands of approaches to a lesson on any given topic at any grade level, you need not limit yourself by planning too far ahead or persisting with one particular method. Before setting up a project with options, however, think through various approaches to consider your needs as well as those of your students. If, for you, student choice parallels opening a door to chaos, avoid open-ended choices and let students pick from several given options. Also, don't offer choice when you are more comfortable with a particular approach to a certain topic. Flexibility should benefit everyone—including you.

When you do present choices to students, provide a structural foundation supporting the choices. That's where rubrics come in. At the beginning of a project, present your expectations, evaluation criteria, and rubrics that define the levels of student achievement. Successful choices start with clear expectations and support.

Student-choice design

At the start of the school year, what if you left one area of your classroom undecorated for students to define and develop? When students have input regarding their surroundings, they gain a sense of ownership, seeing the classroom as much theirs as the teacher's. Offering even one blank bulletin board for students to decorate gives them an immediate sense of involvement and validates their thoughts, tastes, and ideas.

– Jennifer Cole, 4th-Grade Teacher, Horizon
Christian School, Indianapolis, Indiana

Class Jobs

Engage students, enhance their sense of belonging, streamline routines, and teach responsibility by setting up classroom jobs. Class jobs also can coordinate with your classroom economy. With "earnings" from their jobs, students can purchase items at the class store or auction. Post available positions and their pay rates, choosing responsibilities suitable to the age of your students. Give older students a peek into adult life by having them fill out job applications that are rejected if they are messy, filled with spelling errors, or incomplete. Limit lengths of employment to allow students to try different duties.

Job openings

Sharpener of Pencils

Class Custodian

Board Cleaner

Horticulturist (plant keeper)

Messenger

Count/Countess of Lunches

Attendance Officer

Paper Distributor

Class Meetings

Regularly scheduled class meetings offer excellent times to address problems that affect the majority of students in your class and to engage students in meaningful problem solving. To ensure effective meetings, establish clear rules at the first session. Incorporate activities during the meetings and within your classroom to build trust, respect, and community. For a thorough look at class meetings, read books by William Glasser. See **Extras** for suggested titles.

Class meeting dos and don'ts

Dos

- **Do** teach students to use I-statements and to speak in general terms. Avoid using specific names. For example, "I noticed someone cutting in line today," or "I had trouble working because of loud talking."
- **Do** set aside a specific block of time for discussions. The amount of time will vary according to the age of the students.
- **Do** allow anyone to speak who has a concern.
- **Do** facilitate meetings and model procedures during the first few sessions.
- **Do** establish a time limit for the session.

Don'ts

- **Don't** allow students to identify students by names or use put-downs.
- **Don't** ignore or change the meeting time unless absolutely necessary.
- **Don't** let anyone dominate the discussion.
- **Don't** permit foul or disrespectful language or behavior.
- **Don't** allow students to get off track.

Classroom Management Plan

Developing your plan. When you begin developing your classroom management plan, focus first on strategies that encourage and affirm positive behavior. Establish brief, simple rules that help create an environment conducive to learning, accompanied by constructive consequences. Your plan should focus on helping children learn how to manage their own behaviors and reflect your beliefs about learning. The most effective plans usually include student input. Students are more likely to buy into a plan to which they've contributed and that makes sense to them. Besides, you'll be amazed at their great ideas for creating an outstanding learning environment. How you introduce students to the management plan is important, so carefully plan the methods you will use. Students tend to accept governing best when they understand the rationale behind the rules and their consequences. Your management plan also should identify basic classroom procedures. See **Procedures Pave the Way.**

Sharing your plan. Parents need a copy of your classroom rules. Building a partnership with parents begins with clear expectations and knowledge. When they know your rules and the rationale behind them, they are empowered with knowledge about your expectations for their children, and you've helped build trust. The first Open House or Back to School Night is a good time to discuss your management plan.

Don't forget to give your principal a copy of your management plan. Having your plan on file benefits you and the administrators, especially if you have to call upon the principal to back you up on a management issue.

Your students' instructors for art, music, and physical education also need a copy of your management plan. Being aware of one another's rules gives teachers extra eyes and ears. It's amazing how students rarely consider that teachers communicate and share concerns about their students.

Communication

Effective classroom management includes ongoing communication with students and parents. Recurring reports keep parents informed about their child's academic performance and classroom behavior during that long stretch between report cards. Bimonthly or weekly progress reports prevent surprises at report card time for parents and students. See sample on page 84.

Day-to-day charts

Conduct calendars work well for tracking and communicating the behavior of young students. A conduct calendar can be as simple as a monthly calendar (with large boxes for the dates) stapled onto a folder—one for each student. Before the end of the day, quickly assess the student's conduct for that day and mark a symbol (as shown below) on the appropriate date. You may mark the calendar when an incident occurs or wait to assess the day as a whole, a task that can be done quickly while students are preparing for dismissal.

✓+ = Outstanding Behavior   ✓ = Satisfactory Behavior

✓- = Unsatisfactory Behavior

Weekly behavior charts

Charts are a great way to track different behaviors. I use a small spreadsheet for a behavior chart. It streamlines my grading system for work habits and behavior. Each child starts the week with 100 points. For each minor infraction or missing homework, I subtract five points. At the end of the week, each student earns a separate grade for work habits and behavior. The sheet is then sent home along with weekly notes and graded papers. Parents sign it, write notes to me, and return it with their child.

> – Sarah Wolfe, former 2nd-Grade Teacher and current Organizational Staff Development Coordinator for Prince William County Public Schools, Manassas, Virginia

Consequences

Successful classroom management requires that consequences follow broken rules. Valuable consequences incorporate four criteria, according to *Cooperative Discipline* (1990 and 1996) author Linda Albert. They must be **Related, Reasonable, Respectful, and Reliably Enforced.** First, the consequence must be **related** to the offense; there must be a logical connection between the two. Second, the consequence must be **reasonable;** its main purpose should be to teach value rather than punish students. Third, the consequence should be **respectful,** allowing the student to maintain dignity. Last, the consequence must be **reliably enforced** so students know that you stand by your word. It's vital to do what you say you'll do.

Valuable consequence

One annoying and hazardous behavior students commonly exhibit is to rock back in their chairs. Let's say that your student, Justin, is doing just that. You state the problem to him, ask him to stop leaning his chair back, and explain that you don't want him to fall backward and get hurt. If the behavior continues, you then state the consequences that will follow: "Justin, I am concerned about your safety, and if you continue to rock backward, you will lose the privilege of sitting in that chair."

This consequence is **related to the offense** *and a* **reasonable request** from which the child can learn something and maintain dignity **(respectful).** If Justin continues rocking his chair, you must deliver the consequences stated for the rule to become **reliably enforced.** Doing so shows him, as well as other students, that you mean what you say. Consequently, Justin would have to move to another chair, preferably one attached to a desk that cannot rock as easily.

– Pam Kramer, Author of *The ABC's of Classroom Management*

Cooperative Learning

Working with others teaches students how to get along with one another and enhances learning. As you arrange cooperative learning groups, set the stage for success by structuring cohesive units in which each individual clearly understands and is accountable for his or her role and responsibilities.

Once students get used to working cooperatively, you can vary groupings to allow students to work with and learn how to get along with different individuals. Don't worry—those students who cannot and should not

- work together become apparent quickly. For some simple, fun ways to
- group students, see **Grouping Techniques.**

Get out

Conduct a class outdoors if possible. Getting away from the classroom often builds a sense of camaraderie. Encourage teamwork by involving students in group activities such as a scavenger hunt or relay race.

-

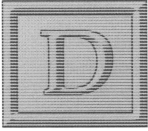

Defiant Students

Insubordinate students challenge you and your self-control; but don't lose your cool! Act rather than react. When a student refuses to follow your directive, pause briefly. Carefully consider

- your response to avoid escalating the circumstances. If not handled properly,
- the situation could become dangerous. Keep your emotions in check and
- avoid engaging in a power struggle with the student. See **Power Struggles.**

- Set a time when you and the student can discuss the defiant behavior privately, allowing sufficient time for cooling down. Make the student aware that though you aren't addressing the behavior at that moment, it will be discussed later. Deliver a firm closing statement that summarizes what happened and the time you plan to discuss the incident. For example, "I understand that you are refusing to sit down at your desk. Is this correct? We will discuss this problem during your morning recess."

- It's very important to remember to deal with the situation at the specified time. When you discuss the problem, analyze events leading up to the problem, and explore ways to prevent recurrences of the problem. Deliver consequences when necessary. If, at any time, you don't feel safe meeting with the student alone, call in the parents, a colleague, or an administrator.

Keepin' it calm

Certain behaviors escalate defiant behavior. Avoid them.

Don't

. . . raise your voice;

. . . use sarcasm;

. . . touch the student;

. . . debate the situation;

. . . stand too close to the student; or

. . . humiliate or mock the student.

Democratic Classroom

- Democracy in classrooms is advocated often, but not always practiced. Student choice, however, can bring democracy to life (also see **Choice**). When you allow students to take part in planning lessons, decorating the room, and solving problems that arise, they experience the democratic process. If two students have defaced school property, for example, they can work together to decide the best way to right the wrong. Problems affecting the whole class should be solved by the whole class (see **Class Meetings**). Though students may not all agree on the same thing at the same time, they can see how working and deciding together can result in a safer, more interesting school life. Your classroom can be the place where students learn they have an important voice—where they learn, from choices made in a classroom setting, how to contribute to society as a whole.

Discipline

Good discipline is a series of little victories in which a teacher, through small decencies, reaches a child's heart.
— Haim Ginott, Teacher, Psychologist, and Child Therapist 1922–1973

Discipline often carries a negative connotation, but it really shouldn't. Carol Charles (2004, 2) defined discipline as "what teachers do to help students behave acceptably in school." Discipline includes both rewards and penalties or consequences. Harry and Rosemary Wong (2004) identified three key components of a discipline plan: rules, consequences, and rewards. Teaching students how to behave appropriately is an essential part of your job. Don't expect that students will enter your classroom with all behavior skills and courtesies mastered. Check **Extras** for resources on classroom discipline.

Displays

Always have student work exhibited in your classroom. Ideally, each student should have representative work on display. Presenting the work about which they are most proud acknowledges students and gives them visibility to others. Recognition through displayed work is especially important to those students who are quiet. When students help determine items to be displayed, you create another opportunity for choice in the classroom.

Emergency Plan

See **Violence** to learn what to do if a student should become violent. Read about preparing for medical emergencies under **Wellness.**

Engagement

Get engaged, no ring required. For this engagement, you need ideas, projects, and creative practices that connect your students to the lessons. When students are engaged in lessons, they focus better, learn more and, therefore, are less likely to misbehave. Though challenging to create, engaging lessons can make a major difference in student behavior and the learning environment.

Hands on

Which objects will sink? Which ones will float? Don't just show and tell—let students test a variety of objects themselves. They will learn more from this engaging activity than any text reading or teacher demonstration. What's more, as actively engaged learners, they are more likely to stay on task while participating.

Environment

From wall décor and colors to desk or table arrangements, various aspects of your classroom influence students and their learning. As director, designer, and choreographer of your classroom stage, it's up to you to create a place that is conducive to learning—where students feel safe and secure. How will you shape that environment?

Start with the room's physical appearance. Is your classroom welcoming and comfortable? Think about the ages of your students and imagine their reactions to the room. Are you concerned about managing the behavior of a few difficult students? Soft colors, particularly blue, tend to be calming. But don't overdo the soothing atmosphere; it still must stimulate students' desire to learn. Add interesting materials and decorations in your classroom that kindle curiosity and promote learning. For suggestions, see *Environment Checklist* in **Extras.**

Next, think about how your personality helps shape the classroom environment. Consider your personal mannerisms. Would students perceive you as friendly, reserved, or withdrawn? Do students sense that you care about them? What does your tone of voice convey? Does it encourage students to listen and speak their minds, or is it sharp or abrupt—a manner that could cause students to be hesitant?

You have the power to create an environment highly conducive to learning. Use that power well. Give respect and you will gain respect.

Expectations

Clearly spell out your expectations for student conduct to prevent poor behavior. Before an activity, such as a cooperative learning lesson, class discussion, or trip through the school halls, give students specific guidelines for behavior. Experienced teachers have seen first-hand how students live up to expectations. See **Preventative Measures.**

Fairness

Fair doesn't mean equal. Fairness comes in many forms but isn't the same as identical treatment. Your job in the learning process is to do what is best for each individual. You will find that being fair is tough to achieve. It's easy to get caught up with the students who are challenging and forget about the attentive and quiet students. Remember that just because students don't demand attention doesn't mean they don't need or want it. "Good" students also need your time and energy.

Fairness is penalizing only the few students who cause a problem rather than delivering a sweeping punishment. Being fair means keeping an open mind. Avoid making assumptions, and give opportunities to all students. Each child must be empowered to have a voice in the classroom. For example, don't assume that a naturally quiet student wouldn't do well giving a speech; some seemingly shy people shine in front of an audience. Also see **Justice.**

Field Trips That Are Fabulous

Planning a field trip is certainly no walk in the park. Careful planning and organization are crucial for a successful field trip. Avoid disasters and conduct a smooth-running field trip using the guide that follows.

Preparation

1. **Plan ahead.** You may find that popular sites are booked more than a year in advance. Before booking a place, check out the site yourself to determine that it is worthy of the time and expense. While there, explore the facility to locate eating areas, restrooms, disabled access, as well as the all-important field trip attraction—the gift shop.

2. **Define the educational purpose** for your trip and indicate that information to administrators and parents at the appropriate times. Purpose and cost are important when you're spending taxpayers' money.

3. **Find and follow the "red tape."** When initiating a field trip, you must know the process and procedures required by your district. Most schools require approval from the principal; some also want school board approval. Find and fill out the proper paperwork and note due dates. Again, planning ahead is essential. At this stage, you'll need to consider the following:
   - Field-trip agenda, which usually is required along with administrative paperwork.
   - Transportation policies.
   - Funding. Who pays—parents, school, special fund, a combination?

4. **Get permission.** What type of permission slips are required by your district? In addition to field trip permissions, you must check the district policy regarding medical emergencies and proper procedures for those children who have special medical needs. Taking children off the school grounds is an awesome responsibility—plan accordingly.

5. **Set a schedule.** Consider these factors when planning the day's agenda:
   - **Lunch or snack.** When, where, and how will students eat? Your site check will help you determine whether students bring a sack lunch or money to purchase food on- or off-site.
   - **Downtime.** Be sure to allow some—but not too much—downtime during the day. You don't want to run ragged the children (or chaperones).
   - **Time frame.** Will the trip fall within normal school hours? If students will return from the field trip after dismissal, determine the arrangement for getting students home. If parents have to pick up their children, they will need to know well in advance.

- **Weather.** Will the field trip take place rain or shine? If not, plan a rain date or backup plan.

6. **Seek volunteer help.** Additional adult assistance is important for successful field trips. Your district's requirements and the type of trip planned will dictate the number of chaperones needed. If the field trip requires chaperones to conduct activities, prepare a study guide or training session for them. When you inform chaperones of your expectations and their responsibilities, they are more comfortable and confident in their roles and more likely to carry out the activity effectively. Taking students on a pond study requires a lot more preparation than taking them on a guided trip through a museum.

7. **Determine your role.** Determine what your role will be during the trip. Will you oversee the event, or will you lead as well as chaperone your own group?

8. **Prepare your students.** In addition to informing students and their parents about what to bring and wear on the field trip, you must prepare students to make curriculum connections from the field trip experience. Field trips are most successful following a unit of study because the students have obtained background content knowledge that the trip can enhance.

9. **Assume nothing.** Plan ahead, follow the *Field Trip Checklist* (see **Extras**), and have directions ready for the bus driver.

Day of the Trip

1. **Double-check necessities.** Make sure you have materials and supplies needed for the trip, as well as emergency contact information, a bag for garbage, and a first-aid kit. If tickets must be purchased, have the needed funds; if you have the tickets already, make sure you've got them with you.

2. **Count.** Count and recount all participants and chaperones.

3. **Keep the schedule.** Start out right; leave on time. If necessary, enlist the help of your chaperones to stay on track.

4. **Enjoy the trip.** Once everyone is on the bus, the count is accurate, and the bus is on the road, relax. Yes, it's possible. You did include ear plugs and a bottle of headache medicine in your supplies, didn't you?

5. **Check-in, and check on.** When you arrive at the site, check-in and register. Let students and chaperones get acclimated to the facility and take a restroom break, especially if the ride was long. Do another head count.

6. **Stay in touch.** Make contact with each chaperone and group throughout the day, in case of changes or problems. Cell phones or walkie-talkies are great when available. Otherwise, appoint check-in times and places a few times during the trip.

7. **Count again.** Prior to leaving the site, settle the students down and do a thorough head count; no child should ever be left behind!

Follow-up

1. **Plan your follow-up.** As a follow-up courtesy, as well as a writing exercise, have students send a thank-you letter to the field-trip site. A more extensive follow-up includes discussion about what the students learned from the trip and making curriculum connections.

2. **Thank volunteers.** Arrange appropriate thank-you messages to chaperones and other volunteers. Let them know that their time and effort are valued.

3. **Push papers.** Submit any necessary receipts or paperwork.

4. **Reflect on the trip.** List aspects of the field trip that worked well along with changes you would make for the next trip.

First-Day Fiasco

Prior planning and backup plans deter day-one disasters. Try these helpful tips from a veteran teacher to make the first day fantastic.

First-day readiness

- Prepare a newsletter for parents introducing you and sharing information about the year ahead. See **Newsletters** and view a sample in **Extras.**
- Make multiple copies of your class and bus lists. Conveniently place them around the room. Copies by the door work as quick checks for fire drills and at dismissal. Also keep copies at your desk for attendance and other record-keeping purposes.
- Post class rules in a prominent spot in your room.
- Hang the lunch menu in an easily seen area.
- Place nametags on desks and in the books of younger students.
- Distribute books and supplies to the students' desks before their arrival. The time saved and the hassle avoided will be worth it.
- Welcome students with preassembled gift bags containing pencils,

stickers, an eraser, and a bookmark. Buying in bulk or from a discount store minimizes the cost.

- Plan a variety of activities and more than enough to get you through the day. These activities should provide essential information and spark students' interest in the upcoming curriculum.
- Read a special book or recite a quote to start the year positively.
- Create a chart noting the date of each student's birthday.
- Determine carefully which classroom manipulatives and supplies you set out on the first day. Keep some of them on reserve so that you have fresh items to bring out later.
- Post the daily schedule, including special classes and events.
- Decorate a hallway bulletin board or a wall outside your classroom door to welcome students.
- Organize those numerous papers that must go home the first day. Individual student folders work well.
- Give yourself a break if things don't go perfectly. Today is only the first day of many; you have tomorrow to do it better.
  — Marge James, 1st-Grade Teacher, East Stroudsburg
      School District, Pennsylvania

First-day viewpoint

Have students express their expectations for the year on the first day. Using a variation of the KWL chart (What We **K**now, What We **W**ant to Know, and What We **L**earned), list what the students know, what they will learn, what they want to study and, finally, what they actually learned. The information can be recorded throughout and at the end of the year.
  — Jennifer Cole, 4th-Grade Teacher, Horizon
      Christian School, Indianapolis, Indiana

Friends Frenzy

Beginning teachers often fall into the friends frenzy with their students— they're bent on being friends with them. It's understandable that you want your students to like you, but don't try to be friends. Doing so is more likely to hinder your effectiveness as a teacher, especially with

- upper-grade students. Your students need you to be their teacher, not
- their best friend. You can be friendly without being their best buddy.
- Show you care, listen, and give advice, but remain the professional adult.
- Don't undermine your ability to exert authority. Once you cross the line,
- it's extremely difficult to step back to the other side.

When a student asked me whether I was her friend, I told her I was her teacher friend.

— Jennifer Cole, 4th-Grade Teacher, Horizon Christian School, Indianapolis, Indiana

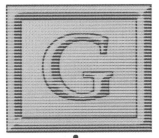

Getting to Know You

Creating community in your classroom requires you and your students to get to know one another as individuals. Becoming acquainted with one another establishes rapport and a sense of belonging. When students believe the teacher perceives them as individuals, and they have a sense of belonging, they are more willing to cooperate.

Learning your students' names as quickly as possible is one of the most important steps you can make to establish community within your classroom. Encourage a comfortable atmosphere by asking students about nicknames and finding out about their interests. Address students by their names as much as possible.

In turn, let students know you. On a Monday morning, share appropriate weekend activities or tell a funny story about your pet. You may want to be the first Star of the Week. Design a bulletin board that introduces you to the class. Bring in personal photographs, samples of hobbies, and favorite artifacts. After introducing yourself, set up a class schedule for Star of the Week to let students share. Rather than bulletin boards, older students may write autobiographies, design a poster, or create an electronic presentation. Sharing allows you to learn about students as they get to know their peers. In addition, you can build community in your classroom with team-building exercises and cooperative learning.

Student sharing

Give students a chance to share news, know one another better, and simply burn off energy with Mara Sapon-Shevin's (1998) "New and Good" game. At a set time weekly, give each person in the room a chance to tell about a recent or upcoming new or good personal experience. Comments must be one- or two-sentence statements to keep the activity from becoming too time-consuming. After sharing "new and good" information, the student passes to another student. However, sharing should be optional.

I first used this activity during student teaching, and the children loved it. To my surprise, the students actually were quite good at keeping their statements concise.

– Jennifer Cole, 4th-Grade Teacher, Horizon
Christian School, Indianapolis, Indiana

Goals

One of the best ways to be an effective classroom manager is to set goals for yourself. Think about what your ideal classroom would be like. What are the most important things you want to accomplish as you manage your classroom? Begin with simple, reasonable goals with high potential for success. Focusing on one goal each day keeps goals manageable. For example, your goal may be to get through the day without raising your voice, and one strategy to achieving that goal may be writing a reminder on a sticky note that you keep with you throughout the day. Support each goal and acknowledge your accomplishment by rewarding yourself when you reach a goal. Celebrate your progress and pick a new goal.

Grading

Like it or not, a good portion of your life as a teacher will be spent grading student work. Yes, it's a time-consuming but essential task for evaluating student progress. To make the most of your time and energy, assess students authentically. Carefully select the tasks you will collect for student grades, offer meaningful and helpful feedback on the finished assignments, and return them to students. Assessment strategies should match lesson goals and objectives. Never assign busy work. Tasks must be meaningful—your time as well as your students' time is valuable. Maintain accurate records on all student work, and save samples of key assignments showcasing growth or concerns.

Grouping Techniques

Some teachers avoid student groups because of hassles they've encountered. This backlash is unfortunate because student groups become wonderful, interactive learning communities when incorporated properly. Using grouping techniques helps students to transition smoothly into group projects, lessons, and games.

Unless there are blatant personality conflicts, group students randomly to produce the most spontaneous and interactive learning ensembles. As students get to know one another, they begin understanding their classmates, and behavior problems become less frequent. Really!

Go with groups

- **Animal antics.** Distribute index cards bearing the name of an animal, according to the group size desired. By making the sound of the animal on their card, students locate and group with the students making the same sound.
- **Candy mates.** Pass out a piece of candy to each student. Students with the same kind of candy form a group. While students love candy mates, you must consider students' allergy and dietary concerns before grouping this way.
- **Famous couples.** Pair students by giving each student an index card bearing the name of one half of a famous couple and instructing students to find the partner (other half). Choose couples appropriate to the age of your students. You may pair with historical matches such as George and Martha Washington or keep it fun and simple with familiar names like Scooby-Doo and Shaggy or Batman and Robin.
- **Musical matches.** Have students find their musical match by humming or singing the song listed on their index cards. Choose widely known songs.
- **Penny pals.** Correlate the number of same-date pennies to the desired group size and distribute a penny to each student. Groups are formed by pennies bearing the same date.

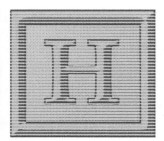

Hand Signals

Save your voice and avoid interrupting classroom flow by using hand signals to obtain or reinforce appropriate behaviors. See **5 simple motions** under **Procedures Pave the Way.**

Health

See **Take Time to** . . . for teacher-related health matters and **Wellness** for information regarding student health records.

Holidays

You will look forward to the fun and vacation time that usually accompanies holidays, but watch out when it comes to classroom management! Students get wound up about a week before holidays and special events. They become easily distracted and noisy, and their level of motivation to do schoolwork sinks to a new low. Wise teachers, which you must be, realize that students won't function at their peak performance during these times. Therefore, don't even think about starting a project or new content. Though class can't be all fun and games, save yourself a lot of frustration and aggravation by planning particularly engaging lessons, such as hands-on activities, to do before the holidays. Appropriately connecting meaningful activities to the holiday theme helps keep students' attention and focus.

Before planning holiday-themed activities, check the school policy concerning holiday celebrations. Your mentor, the principal, or another experienced faculty member can tell you about typical holiday celebrations within the school. Also, be aware of any students who, for religious reasons, are prohibited from engaging in holiday celebrations. Plan non-holiday activities for these children to do or have them visit another classroom during the celebration. Discussing these matters with the parents ahead of time will help you determine your options.

Homework Hassles

Who needs them? You don't and neither do your students. If you set clear expectations about homework from the first day of school, you'll avoid homework headaches. Share your homework policy with students, parents, and your administrator. The policy should include an organized recording system, such as an assignment notebook or journal, and consequences for students who don't do an assignment. Help your students *remember* assignments by posting them regularly in the same places—on the board, class Web site, or the school's homework hotline. Help them *finish* homework by supplying an estimate of the time that the assignment should take and by giving homework that reinforces concepts just learned. Avoid assigning new material that might prove difficult and frustrating to students and parents.

Humor Helps

Humor lessens tension, lightens the mood of the classroom, and lets students see your humanity (see **Be Human**). Laughter is good for the soul, as long as the humor is appropriate. It should never disrespect or ridicule people, especially students.

Even if your friends don't laugh at your jokes, take a walk on the funny side with your students. They are a new audience. Establish a joke of the day, or place a cartoon on the overhead projector at the start of class. Give students a chance to share their favorite jokes—but set joke standards before your first comedian takes stage.

Of course, humor in the classroom isn't limited to jokes. Whim and wit can occur naturally during your interactions with students. Without encouraging student disrespect, laughing at yourself when all doesn't go as planned reduces anxiety and helps students enjoy their time with you.

Ignore Misbehavior

Ignore—and create anarchy? No! In reality, you gain more by ignoring minor infractions rather than confronting petty situations or annoyances over and over again. It's more important to pick your battles than to become a nag whom students tune out. Students who present behavior-management challenges ("troublemakers" in less politically correct and student-centered days) often have a large number of inappropriate behaviors. Disciplining every infraction is virtually impossible—you'd never get to teach! Determine which behaviors most need changing, address them appropriately, and ignore less disruptive misbehaviors. Change doesn't happen automatically or immediately, so start small and work toward manageable goals. Also see **Goals.**

What about the student who won't change behaviors, for whom nothing seems to help? Finding a solution that works is one of the biggest challenges teachers face when dealing with problem behavior. It often takes a great deal of time and effort. When a student presents serious behavior challenges, such as extremely aggressive or violent behavior, involve the parents and administration. Consider consulting a behavior specialist who can develop a specific discipline plan for handling the most difficult behaviors. Some teachers have found successful solutions through Functional Behavioral Assessment (see *Discipline* in the **Resources** section of **Extras** for online information on this approach).

- Never give up on a child, but do recognize when a child
- may need specialized help or another placement. It's not
- your fault, nor have you failed, when you cannot solve all
- of the child's problems. Remember that very challenging
- behaviors usually stem from complex situations that take
- time to resolve.

Every misbehaving child is discouraged and needs continuous
encouragement, just as a plant needs water and sunshine.
    – Rudolf Dreikurs, American Psychiatrist
     and Educator

I-Messages

Use "I-messages" (Gordon 2003) to express concerns to students about their problem behaviors. I-messages are first-person statements about how one feels regarding someone's behavior. As in the example that follows, I-messages are a kinder, gentler means of approaching someone about unacceptable behavior. An I-message first states the problem in a nonjudgmental manner. Next, it identifies what effect the problem has upon you and your feelings about the problem. After that, possible solutions to the problem are discussed. You may feel awkward using I-messages the first few times, but with practice they become excellent communication aids because these nonthreatening statements help students—and adults—become aware of the effects of their behavior on others. *Caution:* Do try this at home!

Sample I-message

"Nick, I feel very annoyed when you speak at the same time I am. When you talk at the same time, neither one of us can be heard by anyone. I have to repeat myself and, consequently, we don't get our work done on time."

Inattentive Students

It's annoying, even aggravating, when students don't listen to what you're saying. You may begin thinking such students are disrespectful. Yet, things aren't always what they seem. Some students look inattentive yet follow everything you say. Others try to listen, but are preoccupied with personal or academic struggles. That students are distracted is not as important as getting them refocused. Whatever reason students are sidetracked, don't let getting them back on task be punitive.

A simple way to gain a student's attention is to use his or her name in an example pertaining to the lesson: "James has a chicken that lays eggs every morning. If his chicken lays 12 eggs and James gives six to the neighbor, how many does he have left?" The first sentence brings James back to reality and gives him a chance to tune in to the actual math problem. Another solution is to use an activity to wake up the student. Ask an inattentive student to demonstrate what you are discussing, participate in a hands-on activity, or run an errand for you.

Is Fun Allowed?

"Start out strict and relax over time" was probably drilled into your head during your teacher training. Experienced teachers know that it's easier to relax than to reestablish discipline, but does that mean you have to be all rules and no fun? Not according to Roxann Kriete (2003), who identified fun as a universal human need. She suggested that when fun is not constructively built into classroom practices, students resort to inappropriate ways to have fun.

Fun is vital to a cohesive classroom community though no guarantee for a trouble-free one. A fun learning environment motivates students internally (Glasser 1998; Erwin 2003), and motivated students are more likely to work hard and behave appropriately. In addition, students are less likely to be stressed and more likely to feel a sense of belonging in an enjoyable environment.

School isn't for entertainment, but when learning and fun can go together, take advantage of it. Games, for example, are a great way to review information and prepare students for tests. Try preparing students for the next science test with a round of *Bingo, Jeopardy,* or *Who Wants to Be a Millionaire?* When the focus is on learning rather than competing, games reenergize students. Also invigorate students by going outside. Play kickball or softball to relieve test anxiety, reward jobs well done, and build community. Bust stress—have fun!

A class that plays together obeys together.
—Anonymous

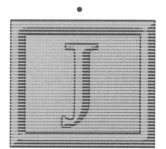

Jellyfish Teachers

Don't get stung by teachers and schools lacking structure, discipline, and backbone that Barbara Coloroso (in Charles 2004) likened to the floating invertebrates that have little control over their destinies. Jellyfish teachers tend to manage inconsistently, failing to provide the structure needed for students to learn responsible behavior. They often drift on low expectations and extremes—swinging from lax rules to harsh and inappropriate measures when students get out of control. Set your feet on solid ground; don't be a jellyfish.

Journey

View each day of teaching as a journey. Think of your teaching as a long trip. Though the destination is a great distance down the road, you will encounter so many new experiences that half of the fun is getting there. So, make stops along the way, see the sights, experience what different places offer, and enjoy the ride. How important is the arrival when you didn't get anything out of the journey?

It's in your head

If you change your mind-set from summer countdown to daily appreciations, the atmosphere of your classroom will change. Students will observe that you value teachable moments more than just getting through the day to the last bell.

— Amy Dyer, Language Arts Teacher, Forest Manor
Middle School, Indianapolis, Indiana

Justice

Often justice is viewed as treating everyone the same. Classroom justice, however, has more to do with recognizing the individuality of your students and interacting with them from that perspective. This characterization of justice is fundamental to successful classroom management. Some students need a little prodding, a few extra minutes, or a few more smiles throughout the day to do what is expected. Striving for across-the-board "fairness" only leads to frustration and stunted learning. Teaching and learning will be far more valuable when you can create a classroom atmosphere that enhances individual potential. Also see **Fairness.**

Individual justice

At the start of the year, have students fill out a profile that asks them biographical information, such as nicknames, hobbies, fears, and favorite movie, book, and childhood memory. When profiles are completed, celebrate those "inequalities" that make each student exceptional—at that time and throughout the year. Justice, the kind students need, will emerge. You might hear the ring of justice when that child who needed the nudge thanks you at the end of the year for all the extra things you did just for her.

– Amy Dyer, Language Arts Teacher, Forest Manor Middle School, Indianapolis, Indiana

Kindness

Try "random acts of kindness" in your classroom; having students perform spontaneous "niceties" for one another is a great cure for interpersonal friction. It's amazing how simple acts of kindness among students change the classroom atmosphere and reduce the number of management problems.

One way that students can show kindness is to write something positive or kind about each student. Supply students with a sheet bearing the class roster to ensure that everyone receives positive feedback. Students then anonymously submit the list to you, and you compile the comments to create and distribute a list for each student. Typically, students are happily surprised at the wonderful comments made by their peers. This idea works well once students have gotten to know one another.

The "Secret Sweetie" award is another way to endorse kindness in the classroom. When you notice students being kind, surprise them with a sweet treat and a brief note thanking them for being kind to others. Silently award students by placing the treat and note on their desks when they are out of the room. Awards like Secret Sweetie are most effective when students are unaware they may be rewarded for their actions.

Kinesthetic

This learning style is often avoided like the plague. Kinesthetic learners require movement, materials, emotion, experimentation—all feared by those who struggle with classroom management. Yet, brain-based research has suggested that many students (especially inner-city, urban children) learn best with kinesthetic-type lessons (Craig 2003). To include activities that promote movement without losing control, set clear and concrete boundaries. State your expectations and accept nothing less. The following is an example of a kinesthetic language arts activity:

1. Group students in threes or fours.
2. Supply one small beach ball per group.
3. Using a permanent marker, write in the colored sections of the beach ball instructional commands such as, "describe, analyze, and compare."
4. In response to your reading, have the students toss the ball to one another. Upon catching the ball, students must respond to the instructional word facing them.

This method stimulates their ability to remember and process information. Don't fear activity in the classroom—wonderful learning can take place in a noisy atmosphere. Read more under **Noise vs. Noisy.**

Location, Location, Location

It's everything in real estate and, believe it or not, in successful classroom management. Optimize your location in the classroom: circulate, circulate, circulate. Too many teachers cling to the front of the classroom, rarely moving about the room as they teach. When you circulate about the classroom, you become aware of what is going on in all areas. In addition, students who are reluctant to ask questions in front of the class are more willing to seek your assistance. Your location helps you keep tabs on students' academic progress and behavior.

Lockers

If your students store coats and books in lockers, let them practice opening and closing their lockers at the beginning of the school year. Working a combination lock the first few times and getting to class on time with the proper materials are challenges that make students anxious. A little extra time at the beginning of the year to get used to a new procedure results in smoother transitions in the long run. Also see **Transitions.**

Lying

Your students must know that lying won't be tolerated in your classroom, but you should understand that lying is somewhat common among children, especially when they're caught doing something wrong. Introduce and remind students that lying is unacceptable by telling them the classroom is a place for respecting one another and that lying is one of the worst forms of disrespect.

Proving that a student is lying is difficult; however, many students "fess up" when direct eye contact is used during a discussion of the problem. Older students who have mastered the art of lying may never admit guilt. Such situations require discernment and careful decision making on your part, based upon the evidence available. When students do admit to lying, acknowledge and praise them for being honest and having the courage to come forward.

Living up to basic, ethical standards in the classroom—discipline, tolerance, honesty—is one of the most important ways children learn to function in society at-large.

– Eloise Salholz, former Senior Writer at *Newsweek* magazine

Motivating the Unmotivated

What if intrinsic motivation doesn't work? Do a little detective work. Observe and talk with the student to discover his or her interests outside of school. Learn about special hobbies, favorite sports, television shows, and games he or she enjoys. Detective work takes time, but it's worth it.

Once you know what interests the unmotivated student, you can reward positive behavior from the student with an activity related to one of those interests. For example, you may play the student's favorite game as a reward for good behavior or genuine effort. Participating in an activity the student enjoys encourages positive behavior and gives you an opportunity to create a bond with the student.

I have thought about it a great deal, and the more I think, the more certain I am that obedience is the gateway through which knowledge, yes, and love, too, enter the mind of the child.
 – Anne Sullivan, Friend and Teacher
 of Helen Keller

Music to Manage By

Songs, poems, and finger plays help younger children transition from one activity to another. A designated passage of music or a stroke across a small xylophone can indicate that it's time to clean up, go to lunch, have story time, or end the day. Play background music during group work. If the music can't be heard, the noise level is too loud.

You also can use music to manage the mood of your classroom. It can calm, soothe, and relax students (and teachers) of any age. If students are wound up from physical education class or recess, try playing soft rock, smooth jazz, or classical compositions to help them settle down. Conversely, when students are restless and off focus, let them dance to faster-paced, rhythmic songs to release their pent-up energy and regain focus.

- Don't overlook the powerful effect of song lyrics as a management tool. Use meaningful lyrics to gain insights, encourage compassion and empathy, and promote class discussion. Kick off a discussion about teasing and cruelty, for example, by playing country singer Mark Will's song "Don't Laugh at Me." Talking about what the song means and how it feels to be made fun of gives insight to those who may not realize how their words and actions affect others.

Names on the Board—**N**ot!

Since the beginning of schools, teachers have written students' names on the board when they misbehave as a reminder to the students and teacher of the offense and its consequence. But how effective is this procedure?

- Students who misbehave probably have self-esteem problems already. Consequently, advertising a student's misbehavior may harm more than it helps. Some students may be humiliated while others may feed on the negative attention. Neither outcome is healthy nor motivating. Why not privately list students who have misbehaved? You can keep accurate records yet respect the students' privacy.

Newsletters

Send a class newsletter home with the students on the first day of school. Introduce yourself, perhaps including your picture, and give an outline of classroom expectations and plans for the year ahead. Continue to send a newsletter regularly throughout the year, having students help with it as much as possible. See a **Sample Newsletter** in **Extras.**

Noise vs. Noisy

You may find it difficult to determine how much noise in a classroom is appropriate. Many novice teachers do. Though your school environment often dictates what a suitable noise level is, a rule of thumb is to gauge whether or not the "hum" of your classroom distracts nearby students or teachers. Obviously, you don't want to disturb others.

As for your personal preference, noise becomes noisy when you feel that the students are getting out of control. Only you can determine that. Especially during your first year, it's very important that your classroom functions at a level in which you feel in control.

Caution: If you prefer silence most of the time, you need a reality check! Students are human beings, after all, who are social creatures. Expect noise during group work and projects. Sharing knowledge and ideas is inherent in the process of learning. Ensuring that students stay on task while conversing is your challenge.

Turn down the volume!

Devise a signal that lets students know to get quiet immediately. Introduce and practice it the first week of school. The type of signal you choose doesn't matter, only that students know what it means. Many teachers use one of these:

- Raise a hand or an index finger.
- Turn off the lights.
- Clap a rhythm.
- Ring a bell.
- Call out a catch phrase such as "give me five" to which students respond by raising five fingers in the air.

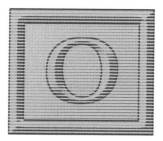

One Size Doesn't Fit All

No one single style works every time when it comes to classroom management. If you teach more than one group of students, don't be surprised when a strategy that works like magic with one class bombs with another. Not all students respond alike. Effective classroom management is a work-in-progress—a plan tweaked and honed during the year and throughout your career. Be open to adjusting your approach for different types of students, and don't give up on the first try. Plan ahead, but realize that trial and error often become your greatest teachers.

Organization

Entire books (see **Resources** under **Extras**) are written on getting organized. They're written because organization of plans, materials, and time leads to successful management of your day, whether you're a first-year teacher or a veteran. When you don't plan well, too much time and energy is lost on daily tasks. Alleviate problems before they start by building your management plan on a foundation of organization.

Daily tasks

- Prepare all lesson handouts, manipulatives, and materials before class. Make sure they are easily accessible during instruction.
- Put up a morning assignment for students to begin shortly after arriving and settling in the classroom.
- Post the day's schedule to give students a heads-up on the day's activities.
- Write out an inspirational quote or comic the same place you post assignments to help establish the classroom mood.
- Jot down observations about individual students throughout the day using sticky notes. Later, stick those notes in the student files or record your observations electronically.
- Have students carry out set routines.

Long-standing tasks

- Establish an efficient procedure for collecting and distributing papers and supplies to prevent students from getting off-task during these times. Whether you use a particular routine or assign a student to the task (see **Class Jobs**) doesn't matter as long as your system is orderly enough to become a routine.
- Designate a drop-off zone where students place homework and pick up important papers. Centrally located In and Out baskets work well for this process.
- Create individual student mailboxes for the delivery of important papers.
- Use take-home folders for homework and papers, especially for younger students. Take a two-pocket folder, label the left side **Left** for things to be *left at home;* the right side **Right** for things to come *right back.*
- Create individual student files to keep work samples, important notes, papers, observations, and other record-type items that will keep you well informed for parent conferences, report cards, and phone calls to parents. Log and date each item placed in a folder, as well as any communication with parents and administrators about the student.
- Develop a system to monitor attendance. Calling out names lets you greet students individually along with taking attendance. Having students sign in or turn in a homework folder as they arrive also monitors attendance.

Organize it

Daily handouts. Purchase a filing system with compartments for each day of the week. Place all copies to be used on a particular day in its corresponding compartment. Check your plans at least three days ahead of time to have enough time to get copies made.

Supplies. At the end of each month, inventory your classroom supplies to ensure adequate materials for the next month. Maintain a list of all ordered and used supplies from the beginning of the year. The month's end is also a good time to change bulletin boards.

IEP papers. Students with special needs have individualized education plans guiding their instructional abilities and needs. You must follow the IEP and document work accomplishing its goals, so prepare a file on each student with an IEP. Set a goal to update these files at least weekly, if not daily; making time to record evidence regularly is far easier than playing catch up. Store the confidential IEP files in a safe place.

Unit materials. Store materials related to a particular unit of study together. Following your rain forest unit, for example, place the bulletin board materials, resources, artifacts, sample projects, and associated children's literature in a clearly labeled container. Include an inventory sheet of the contents. The next time you teach the unit, you'll have what you need. You can always add or refresh contents, but you won't have to start over or spend an excessive amount of time searching for what you need.

Outcasts

Sadly, almost every class has at least one outcast or social misfit who just isn't accepted by the other students. All too often, this student becomes the source of jokes, mocking, and mistreatment. It is up to you to help students realize that such behavior will not be tolerated in your classroom. Realize that as much as you may love children, you will have students who are difficult to connect with or who have irritating behaviors, odors, and personality traits.

Therefore, before discussing your students' behaviors toward the "social misfit," examine your own attitude. How do you treat the student? What do you communicate, verbally and nonverbally? Students are incredibly perceptive, easily picking up on your feelings about particular students. Count that among your reasons to model respect and dignity for every student. When incidents regarding the misfit student do occur, take immediate action to make it clear that inappropriate treatment of students is not allowed. Looking the other way only increases problems.

Bringing the out, in

Encourage acceptance and respect of the social outcast in your classroom by helping students see him or her in a more positive light. Showcase a special talent or ability, or call upon a well-liked student to show respect for this student as an example for others to follow. Consult the school guidance counselor for suggestions and assistance.

Parents

Promote parents as partners with special activities such as **Family Science Night.** Check out the guidelines for this event in **Extras.** For more information about communicating with parents, see **Relationship Building.**

Parent–Teacher Conferences

See the *Parent-Teacher Conference Preparation Checklist* in **Extras.**

Patience

It's touted as a virtue, but when it comes to classroom management, it's a necessity. Even veteran teachers struggle from time to time, so don't beat yourself up if you wrestle with managing your classroom. Be patient— with your students and with yourself.

You must first have a lot of patience to learn to have patience.
– Stanislaw J. Lec, Author

Power Struggles

Avoid power struggles with students; they are no-win situations. If a student taunts you with a verbal or nonverbal message of "You can't make me," don't get drawn into proving it—because you really can't. When our authority is threatened, the human response is to flex our muscles and fight back. Don't! It's the surest way to lose authority. Check your first reaction and respond calmly. You are the professional.

If a boy refuses to sit down after being asked, for example, debating the issue—especially in front of the class—will get you nowhere. Instead, firmly tell the student that he can choose to sit down now or see you after class. It may seem as though you are surrendering to his wishes by delaying action; however, holding out will result in later victory (see **Defiant Students**). When a student is particularly disruptive, have him or her accompany you to the hallway for a controlled, but firm, discussion.

Power whisper

Speak softly (and carry no stick) to get a student under control. Standing close to a student and speaking softly, so that only the student can hear, effectively brings about better behavior.

Preventative Measures

As you plan lessons and activities, anticipate potential snags in your plans, and prepare for those as well. For example, if you know that Josh and Kayla tend to bicker with each other, avoid placing them in the same group. Perhaps you've been forewarned about a possible fire drill "sometime next week." Take advantage of that knowledge and build flexibility in your schedule, especially if your lessons include a science experiment or test.

An ounce of prevention is worth a pound of cure.
— Henry de Bracton, English Writer

Principles for Dealing with Principals

How do you know when to send a child to the principal? Your first and foremost guide should be your school's discipline policy; refer to and rely on it. When a major policy is violated, you should notify the principal or other appropriate administrator. Severe problems, such as violent behavior, threats, serious bus issues, and weapon-related concerns, must always be reported immediately. If you're unsure about a difficult issue not outlined in the school handbook, consult your mentor or another trusted colleague. Otherwise, managing classroom behaviors is in your hands. Maintaining control of your class on your own builds your confidence and displays your competence to students, administration, and colleagues.

When a student's poor behavior continues, be sure to collaborate with the parents before involving the principal. Parents know their child best and can offer strategies they've found helpful. Work with them to develop solutions for managing their child. To encourage open lines of communication, always keep parents informed of ongoing behavior problems even when no major violations of school policies occurred. If parents aren't responsive, or they place the responsibility entirely on you, talk with your principal immediately.

Prioritizing

Many well-organized teachers who comfortably juggle various responsibilities still find themselves struggling to keep up with paperwork, lesson planning, and messages via voice mail and e-mail. So, should you find yourself overwhelmed with messages, IEP reports, papers to grade, and faculty memos, try some of these tips for prioritizing:

- After picking up your mail, begin separating out the junk mail as you return to your classroom.
- Sort your mail next to the garbage can or recycling bin. Toss junk mail, unopened, into this file-13 receptacle.
- Throw out mail that you've looked at but don't need to address.
- Separate the remaining mail into three baskets: Immediate Attention, Do This Week, and File.
- Sort e-mails similarly. Delete junk mail and respond immediately to as many e-mails as you can.
- Place messages to be addressed later into a file marked as such.
- Check e-mail messages at a designated time daily.

Problem Solving 101

Solving problems isn't your job alone. Students can and need to learn how to seek positive resolutions to problems. Don't expect that they already have the skills to do so, though. No matter what age your students are, start with basic skills in conflict resolution, guiding them and practicing techniques until they understand. For additional sources on problem solving, check **Resources** under **Extras.**

Syllabus for Problem Solving 101

1. Identify the problem. Allow individuals involved to share their feelings and needs about the situation.
2. Brainstorm possible solutions to the problem.
3. Evaluate solutions individually using the question, "What would happen if?"
4. Select what is thought to be the best solution and try it.
5. Monitor that solution; continue using it or seek a new one.

Procedures Pave the Way

Procedures or routines are the first line in classroom management. They outline expected student behaviors for various activities in the classroom upon which you can build a cooperative community. When you establish routine procedures for student movement, topic or class transitions, non-instructional tasks, materials management, and group work, behavior management is built into your classroom. The key to effectively followed procedures is to establish clear-cut routines from the first day of school and to practice, practice, practice them.

When introducing a procedure, tell students the exact consequence of not following the procedure properly and have them practice the routine. Time spent in practice is worth it in the long run. Further reinforce a procedure by having students verbally reiterate each step involved. Common procedures include:

Arrival and dismissal routines

If you love beginning and ending the day chaotically, don't plan these routines! If, however, you prefer an orderly beginning to the school day and a relatively smooth student exodus at the end of class, establish specific procedures for students to follow. Upon arrival, students must quickly put away their coats and books, turn in homework, and prepare for the day ahead, which may include sharpening pencils. A posted assignment settles students into the classroom while deterring off-task socializing. The reward for students promptly accomplishing the morning routine could be student-choice reading time.

Dismissal times can be the most chaotic; therefore, the first rule to implement is that you—not the bell—must dismiss students. When that bell rings, students want to charge out the door. If it's been a tough day, you might welcome such an exit. Inevitably though, students will take off without homework, backpacks, mittens, or even their coats. Set up orderly routines for gathering books, projects, papers to go home, and personal items. Stick to those routines, and you and the students will go home happier.

Fire drills

Follow your school's policy for fire drills, but prepare your students for what they must do and where they should go in case of an emergency. Periodically walk through these procedures to instill them in students should such an emergency occur. Always keep a class roster handy to help you account for all students during drills and emergencies. Place this roster in an obvious place, such as by the door.

Materials management

Established procedures for distributing, collecting, and storing instructional materials allow students to complete these tasks easily and efficiently.

Other non-instructional tasks

Set procedures so that students can help you take attendance, collect permission slips, do participation counts, and keep the classroom neat.

Restroom and water fountain breaks

What procedure will work best for your classroom—all students taking a break at one time or individually leaving the room as needed? If you allow students to leave the room as needed, how will they obtain permission? Some teachers set up a hand signal that students use for permission to leave the room without interrupting the whole class. Other teachers post a sign-out sheet to avoid interruptions and to document the frequency of these breaks.

Transitions

Help students transition smoothly to the next lesson or activity by organizing instructional materials and instructions in ways that allow students to get started on their own. Listing necessary materials on the daily schedule is one method to achieve this direction.

5 simple motions

Each of the following procedures has a corresponding hand motion that I use to signal the desired behavior. Signals let me avoid interrupting instruction or pointing out a particular student. The kinesthetic reminder reinforces the expectation. I hang a poster of these procedures accompanied by pictures of students doing the corresponding motions. These procedures work well because students have been reminded verbally, visually, and kinesthetically. Eventually, a verbal reminder becomes unnecessary, and students use the signals to politely remind one another.

1. **Follow directions.** Extend your pointer finger straight up into the air and make a circular motion.
2. **Listen.** Show two fingers, then make an L shape with your thumb and pointer finger, and put it up to your ear.
3. **Raise your hand.** Show three fingers and raise your hand above your head.
4. **Keep your hands and feet to yourself.** Show four fingers, shake hands, point to feet, and cross arms.
5. **Never hurt anyone on the inside or the outside.** Show five fingers and then shake your head while pointing to your heart and out toward the audience.

   – Erika Lee, Kindergarten Teacher, Aurora Public Schools, Aurora, Colorado

Project-Based Learning

Using the constructivist approach for instruction changes your role and the classroom environment itself. You are not so much an instructor as a facilitator helping students develop their ideas and gather materials necessary to complete their projects. Expect noise and movement in a project-based learning environment as students accomplish common goals together. Curb noise levels with strategies found in **Noise vs. Noisy.**

Proximity Control

Placing easily distracted students near you helps them work more productively. That proximity also allows you to monitor individual progress. When circulating about the classroom, be sure to make frequent stops by those students who are easily sidetracked or needy. Often a

-
-
-
-

teacher's physical presence prevents students from misbehaving. If an incident arises, you can readily handle it privately.

Quick-and-Easy Attention Grabbers

With a room full of students, obtaining everyone's attention on short notice can be difficult. That's why teachers use quick attention grabbers to quiet students immediately.

-
-

To ensure the success of your attention grabber, teach your students its meaning and the expected response to the given signal. See **5 simple motions** under **Procedures Pave the Way** for one teacher's silent attention grabbers.

-

Your attention please

- Turn off the lights.
- Clap a rhythm.
- Hold one hand in the air.
- Ring a bell.
- Say "Freeze."
- Develop an acronym or phrase that means to stop and listen. The Wongs (2004) suggested SALAME: **S**top **A**nd **L**ook **A**t **ME.**
- Play a short musical passage. Sound three notes or make a stroke across a xylophone. See **Music to Manage By** for more ideas about using music as a management tool.
- Say "All eyes on me."
- Blow a horn or whistle, especially in physical education settings.

-

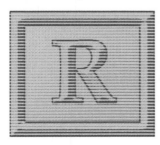

Reflection

See **Take Time to . . ..**

-

Relationship Building

With students. Marzano and Marzano (2003) found that teachers who had strong relationships with their students had fewer discipline problems than teachers who did not. They suggested the following habits to build positive relationships with students:

- Greet students when they arrive to class, using their names when you greet them.
- Compliment students (haircut, clothes, important achievements).
- Attend extracurricular activities. Your students will be thrilled that you took the time to come see them.
- Talk to students informally whenever possible.
- Ask questions about their interests.
- Listen, listen, listen!

Special treatment

Students like to feel special, so when I taught second grade, I included activities in the classroom routine that promoted personal attention, fun, or distinction to build relationships with my students. Those exclusive activities included:

- **Executive lunches with students.** Individual or group lunches forge a special bond between you and the students. I used a tablecloth or place mats to emphasize the special occasion.
- **Student surveys.** My students had fun developing surveys and polling their peers on likes and dislikes.
- **Individual reading or writing conferences.** One-on-one conferences are a great way to connect with each student.
- **Journal dialogues.** I not only read students' journal entries and personal narratives, but also wrote comments back to students.

  – Sarah Wolfe, former 2nd-Grade Teacher and
    current Organizational Staff Development
    Coordinator for Prince William County Public
    Schools, Manassas, Virginia

With parents. Though building relationships with parents may take extra effort on your part, it is effort worth making. Partnering with parents may be the key to helping a struggling student, acquiring that extra hand for a class project, or having enough parents for a special field trip. To develop rapport with parents, use approaches similar to those used with students. One idea is to ask parents to write a letter to you about how their child is special. To encourage response, consider assigning the letter as homework at back-to-school night. Bribe them with homework passes for their children when the letter is returned within a week's time.

Recipe for successful communication with parents

2 cups of patience

2 cups of humility

2 ears for listening

1 heaping of nonjudgmental attitude

2 cups of love

2 cups of respect

2 cups of wisdom

Mix ingredients well with understanding and a willingness to do what's best for the child. Serve extra-large portions.

Even a great recipe may not lead to perfect results, but when establishing good rapport with parents, you can't go wrong starting out with ample portions of the best ingredients.

The only reason I always try to meet and know the parents better is because it helps me to forgive their children.
— Louis Johannot, Headmaster,
Institut Le Rosey, Switzerland

With the principal. Develop a good rapport with your principal, and you'll be at ease going to him or her with questions or difficult classroom situations. Communicate professionally. Sharing your concerns about difficult behaviors with the principal helps equip him or her to support your management techniques.

Rewarding Positive Behavior

Whether or not to reward appropriate behavior is a very personal, philosophical question you must determine for yourself. According to research evidence from the field of psychology, humans tend to repeat rewarded behaviors. From retail rebates to good behavior parties in the classroom, reward systems are common in Western society. Despite this trend, some teachers believe that rewarding good behavior is merely bribing students to do what they should do anyway. Not sure what you want to do? Check *Rewards* under **Resources** in **Extras** for books and articles on the subject.

As you consider the pros and cons of rewarding behavior, keep in mind that intangible rewards tend to be effective. A positive phone call to parents, a word of encouragement, or an unexpected reward can be valuable. In fact, unexpected rewards work best. Varying what and when you reward keeps students on track because they never know when they might be rewarded. Continual rewards lose their motivating power and may actually encourage Greed Monsters—students who won't make an effort unless a reward is involved.

If you decide to reward good behaviors, avoid focusing on immediate gratification or material returns. Plan out the type and frequency of rewards you will use. Start small and keep them simple, corresponding rewards and behaviors; don't reward commonly expected behaviors with grandiose rewards. When not overdone, stickers and prizes can be constructive, especially for young students. If you choose against tangible rewards, develop a plan for motivating students to follow the rules. Positive comments and gestures augment any reward system and serve well as intangible rewards. Smile when students display good behavior. Thank them for their efforts. Give them a thumbs-up now and then along with literal or figurative pats on the back. When praising students for jobs well done, point out a specific attribute of their work. Who wouldn't benefit from genuine and deserved feedback?

Rules

For a classroom that functions effectively, you must establish "expectations of appropriate student behavior" (Wong and Wong 2004,

143). The Wongs strongly recommended numerous procedures as the infrastructure of classroom management anchored by three to five core classroom rules. A short list of rules is easy to remember and follow; so establish just a few critical rules for classroom behavior and let procedures help manage the rest (refer to **Procedures Pave the Way**). Whether you form the rules or you allow your students to help establish them, introducing rules during the first few days of the school year is essential. Set clear expectations and post the rules as a reminder.

Listing behaviors you don't want from students is easy, but what a long list that might be! Besides, "Don't" lists, by their very nature, are negative and may give students an excuse for a poor behavior simply because it wasn't listed. Instead, take a proactive approach by listing positive expected behaviors. Reasonable and fair rules that support self-responsibility empower students and increase the likelihood of having followers.

Broken rules—even positive and proactive ones—must have consequences to be effective. Students are human (even when they act like they're from another planet), so broken rules are inevitable. How you handle infractions greatly influences the success of the rules. Effective consequences directly connect to rules in a manner that is logical and meaningful to students. Students must understand the connection for them to resume following the rules and managing their own behavior appropriately. Also see **Consequences.**

Rule box
+ and − rules
Don't call out. (Negative)
Raise your hand when you have something to share. (Positive)

Cause and effect
Broken rule: A student fails to raise her hand to speak.

Appropriate consequence: Teacher ignores what the student said and calls on someone else to respond.

Inappropriate consequence: Teacher sends the child to the principal.

Seating Charts

Learn your students' names quickly with the aid of a seating chart. It's a must if you teach more than one group of students. Using small sticky notes for students' names on seating charts allows you to make quick and easy changes. Keep the seating chart intact by covering it with a clear protector sheet.

Stealing

Don't be shocked if stealing occurs in your classroom. Though unacceptable behavior, stealing is not uncommon among children. When incidents of stealing occur, use them as learning opportunities on the difference between right and wrong. Focus on the idea that your class is a community where each person is respected and trust is important.

If something is stolen in your classroom, tread carefully; proving theft is difficult. Sometimes students declare that an object has been stolen, only to discover later that they misplaced it. If a student is found with a missing object, he or she is likely to claim that the object was borrowed. Often students simply don't admit guilt out of fear for what will happen to them.

Rather than getting caught up in proving stealing and possibly escalating the situation, you might make a general request for the item to be returned as soon as possible. Having students anonymously return the alleged stolen goods lets them save face, yet correct their actions and do what is right. If the identity of the light-fingered borrower is known, be sure to address the issue privately.

No matter how disappointed you feel, try to deal with the problem without letting your emotions interfere. Also, keep public knowledge of the incident to a minimum.

— Thomas O. Jewett, Assistant Professor,
McKendree College, Lebanon, Illinois

Students with Special Needs

Accommodating students with special needs applies to classroom management as well as academics. Work closely with your building's special education professionals and parents to develop the best behavior-management plan for these students. A student's Individualized Education Plan (IEP) should guide your efforts to help the child manage his or her behavior responsibly.

Children with behavior disorders may challenge you, but they still deserve your respect and care. When these students act out, be patient with them and yourself. Try not to take the misbehavior personally; think of their actions as bad behavior rather than viewing these students as difficult children.

Special concerns

To learn about specific behavior-management systems that have been successful for students with special needs, search the Web site of the Council for Exceptional Children *(www.cec.sped. org)*. The CEC is the major advocacy group for special education professionals.

Take Time to . . .

. . . care for yourself. Seems obvious, doesn't it? Yet burnout (see **Burnout**) can happen easily in the teaching profession. The first year, especially, can be overwhelming. When you step into the classroom, you become a facilitator of learning while still learning so much yourself. On-the-job training is inherent in any first-time position, but you also are establishing competency and comfort levels with students, colleagues, parents, administrators, and curriculum. For these reasons, veteran teachers recommend self-care to ensure a balanced lifestyle.

Veteran teachers also must care for themselves. Working in a service profession can be demanding, and many teachers tend to put their own needs last. Be sure to take time to care for yourself so that you retain the energy and dedication to continue helping others.

Self-care tips

1. **Seek mentors and resources.** Collaborate with your mentor for help in thinking through possible solutions to educational challenges. Investigate Web sites, education-related online bulletin boards, books, and articles for ideas, solutions, and connections.

2. **Nurture emotional health.** Focus on positive activities and solutions that will help solve problems and emotionally recharge you. Sharing emotions can be a helpful release, but do so carefully. Remain professional by talking privately without mentioning identifying information. Enjoy your life outside of work.

3. **Sustain physical health.** Whether you walk, jog, kickbox, garden, or dance, take time each week for physical activity to boost your immune system, mental sharpness, productivity, and overall well-being.

4. **Support mental health.** As simplistic as it seems, sometimes mind over matter is the best solution to challenges and frustrations. To prevent getting bogged down in situations, train yourself to look at difficulties as challenges—as professional puzzles in need of creative solutions. Look for positive qualities in each student and colleague, and be sure to document and celebrate successes.

– Adapted from an article by Andrea Sabatini
McLoughlin, *New Teacher Advocate,* Fall 2003

. . . reflect on the effectiveness of your management strategies. Whether you write your observations in a journal to read through at a later date, videotape yourself teaching a lesson, or discuss lessons and techniques with colleagues, reflection is vital to professional and personal growth. Considering your classroom practices and student responses in an objective manner is critical to ongoing learning—both yours and your students'.

Reflective questions

- Are students improving their self-control?
- Do respect and community characterize your classroom?
- Are rules being followed?
- Is your classroom an effective learning environment?

If you answered "no" to any of the reflective questions listed here, dig deeper to discover what prevents achievement of that goal in your classroom. Writing down what you did right and what you did wrong can help you learn from mistakes. When you have feelings of failure, keep mistakes in perspective—view them simply as new learning experiences. You may need someone else to help you gain perspective and clarity. Your mentor, or a trusted colleague, could observe you in the classroom and give you feedback.

Getting perspective

- Set goals for instructional, professional, and personal growth.
- Connect with colleagues and find a mentor.
- Communicate with your principal.
- Get involved with the school and community.
- Keep a journal of your great lessons—and the not-so-great ones, too—for developing future lessons.
- Make time for sharing and planning.

> – Sarah Wolfe, former 2nd-Grade Teacher and
> current Organizational Staff Development
> Coordinator for Prince William County Public
> Schools, Manassas, Virginia

Tattling

It can try a sane person's patience! At the primary or elementary level, however, it comes with the territory. Young children tend to tattle and may even believe that telling on someone is actually the right thing to do—and it can be when someone is hurt or involved in a dangerous situation. One apt report, however, often turns into a string of tattling on everything others have done wrong. Totally eliminating tattling is unrealistic (sorry!), but you can tame the torrent. Here are a few suggestions for managing tattlers:

- When a student begins to tattle, stop him or her and ask, "Is anyone hurt?" If not, send the student back to work it out with that person.
- Assign a peer mediator. Encourage responsibility in students by having them discuss the situation with a student who serves as a mediator, listening to the individuals involved and helping them resolve their problem. Because most incidents that trigger tattling occur during recess, lunch, or independent work time, a peer mediator can be a great resource.
- Hold a regular class meeting at least once per week—more often, if needed—during which students may share their tattles. Usually, the problem has been forgotten by meeting time.
- Give mini-lessons on getting along with others and resolving problems. Share stories representing these topics and provide activities that develop interpersonal skills.

Tattletale

Many young students find it difficult to resist the urge to be first to let the teacher know who's done what. Because of that tendency, some teachers place a Book of Tattles in their rooms. Rather than running to the teacher with a tattle, students write out the tattle in a notebook that the teacher views later.

Teacher Look

Get it. Use it. Never underestimate the power of nonverbal communication—it's very effective in classroom management. A well-timed pause along with direct eye contact tells students that you mean business, and most students quickly stop misbehaving when they get the look. Do you have the teacher look? Practice it.

Testing

Students often become anxious about tests, especially standardized tests that extend over several days. Some test anxiety comes from not knowing what to expect. To ease students' fear of the unknown, familiarize them with the format of the test ahead of time so they can concentrate on content during actual testing. Use the samples provided by the testing companies for that purpose. Help students cope with the pressure of being timed by giving practice timed tests and encouraging a sense of rising to a challenge rather than fearing the "ticking clock."

When testing time comes, encourage your students to eat a good breakfast. Parents might be willing to send in wholesome snacks as a special treat. Prepare yourself by becoming familiar enough with the test's format and directions to remain calm and in control as you administer the test. Answering students' questions clearly and confidently reassures them. Incorporate into the days of testing tension-releasing activities, such as stretches, deep breathing exercises, calisthenics, and outdoor games to give students an outlet and help them focus on the test. At the end of the day's testing, acknowledge their efforts with a special activity, such as extra recess time, a class kickball game, relay races, or a walk outside the building.

Time Out

If any management strategy is overused and abused, it's Time Out. Doled out too frequently, Time Out loses its value and effect. For Time Out to be significant, Time In must be more appealing. A student placed in Time Out for misbehaving during grammar drills probably celebrates a victory! Being sent to Time Out during a favorite math game is a greater hardship. Time Out removes a student from a group activity with the purpose of regaining self-control and composure for eventual return. The more appealing Time In, the greater motivation a student has to regain self-control. When a student is to return to the group, first ask whether he or she is ready to return and act appropriately. The student can't return unless the response is clearly positive. Make a student's return to Time In a nonevent—a quick welcome without scolding or negativity.

Time-savers

Grading. When appropriate, have students grade their own papers during class time. Set up a few pass/zero assignments in which successfully completed assignments receive a passing grade and incomplete assignments get a zero. Give partial points to partially completed assignments. For less tedious grading, divide writing assignments and long projects into several small steps. See **Grading.**

Paperwork. Daily classroom life is overflowing with papers. Assignment notebooks, binders, student mailboxes, and plastic crates are all proven tools for helping students get organized. Consider using some of these organizational ideas yourself to keep track and organize the flood of papers.

Technology. Save time, save a tree—go electronic. As much as possible, keep records and communicate with colleagues and parents electronically. Embrace technology and record grades on your computer. Send notes to parents via e-mail or the class Web site, but take care to find an alternative for parents who don't have access to computers. Make use of a homework hotline. Spend a little bit of time searching recommended Web sites for ideas, experiments, and lesson plans to incorporate into your curriculum, and develop lesson plans on the computer. Do you have students more tech savvy than you? Don't be intimidated; learn from them.

Paperwork pointer

Monthly paper files, subdivided into days (1–31), keep me organized. When a form, notice, e-mail, or letter comes in that must be addressed later, I file it in the appropriate date. Then I add a reminder to my planner. My notes include details. For example, if I get word that an assembly is scheduled for May 17 in the gym and my class is to leave at 9:04 and sit in row 5, I jot "9:04 to gym" in my planner or PDA and place the notice describing the event in the file. Each day, I pull the next day's file folder to keep on my desk as reference.

–Theresa Knipstein Meyer, 2000 Milken National Educator

Transitions

Moving students from one class or subject to another doesn't just happen. You must plan strategies to ensure smooth transitions. Advance warnings are important. Forewarn students about an upcoming change to give them a few minutes to finish what they are doing and gather their materials. Timing is crucial. You don't want a classroom of students impatiently waiting in the hallway for another class to exit your room. Unexpectedly rewarding students when they quickly and quietly gather their books and supplies encourages that behavior in the future.

Elementary changes

Music. Use music to cue students about a change. Play or sing a specific song that signals a transition.

Clapping sequence. Teach students to copy your clapping sequence. When you clap, you command their attention while signaling a transition.

Undesirable Behaviors

When students continually exhibit unacceptable behaviors, there is an underlying reason. Whether an irritating habit, aggressive behavior, or lying, the student reaps a benefit from it. Essentially, four psychological elements drive student misbehaviors: attention, power, revenge, and inadequacy (Dreikurs, Cassel, and Ferguson 2004).

Determining which element drives your student's misbehavior is your challenge, because recognizing the motivating need behind the misbehavior helps you gauge a proper response without fulfilling the sought-after need. Look for clues to help the student learn healthy alternatives in getting his or her needs met. Students who misbehave simply to get *any* type of attention should receive attention only when they don't act out. Watch for positive behavior from these students and

- make a point to compliment them. Offer a word of praise, for example,
- when one of these students uses proper manners, shares a snack, or
- uncharacteristically raises his or her hand before speaking.

Unresponsive Parents

- It's frustrating when you need parents' help in meeting their child's needs
- and they are unresponsive. Informing the parents as much as possible
- about their child's progress and behavior becomes even more important
- when parents are uninvolved. You may question why you should try
- so diligently when the parents don't, but continue your efforts anyway.
- Call, send notes or e-mails, and set up mini-conferences to discuss your
- concerns. You never know when your perseverance will pay off. What's
- more, you may be the only one standing in that child's corner.

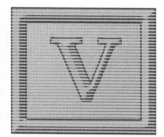

Violence

Violence is every teacher's nightmare. When faced with the threat of violence, your first responsibility is to ensure the safety of the students in your classroom. Don't try to be
- a hero or martyr, but do everything possible to keep the students safe.
- Know your school's policy for dealing with violent behavior so that
- you won't be caught off guard. Aside from the process outlined by your
- school, there is no one step-by-step formula for dealing with violence
- because each situation is different. However, remaining calm, using
- common sense, and having patience are the best lines of defense.

- At the first sign of a violent reaction, concentrate on being composed;
- agitating the offender will only escalate the situation. Calmly, but firmly,
- talk the student into settling down and refraining from a violent act. If a
- weapon is involved, keep your distance and don't make any quick moves.

- If possible, get the other students out of the classroom or at least away
- from the offender. Work out an emergency plan that includes a signal
- between you and a few students that cues someone to go for help. A
- specific phrase, code, or motion is important in potentially unstable
- situations. The volatility of the situation should determine the practicality

63

of such an action, but an initial plan is valuable. Remaining collected is the best approach when attempting to get the offender to calm down or release a weapon. As you wait for help, keeping the offender talking can deter further violent actions.

No matter which strategies your school district uses, or is planning for reducing the threat of violence, you can employ techniques within your classroom to shape a nonthreatening community. Establish a positive and caring learning environment where differences are respected, guiding students to realize what that means to them personally. Help them learn to trust and to give respect. Also, let students know that they can come to you when they need help. If you suspect that a student may be involved in a gang or violent behavior, share your concerns with the proper authorities as required by school and civil policies. Report any student who seems increasingly angry or who loses control frequently or with mounting aggression. Intervention may be necessary.

When a student acts violently

1. Immediately command the student to stop.
2. Using his or her name, command the student to sit down.
3. Ensure the safety of other students. If necessary, send them out of the room. Also consider your own safety by putting distance between you and the offending student, but continue telling the student precisely what to do.
4. Get help controlling the student from an administrator, school security, or the police.
5. Follow preestablished consequences and corrective actions as well as school policies regarding violent behavior.
6. Document the incident completely and duplicate copies of the report.
7. Arrange for the student to get special help with anger management.

Volunteers

So many teachers want help in their classroom, yet they often see volunteers as more work for them! Don't miss out on extra hands in your classroom—plan ahead for volunteers. Preparation is the secret to having willing volunteers and productive results. When you take the time to set up specific projects or ongoing activities with accompanying instruction sheets, volunteers can jump into working and you won't have to be pulled from your teaching. Another way to train volunteers is to offer periodic training sessions for particular activities such as math evaluations or one-on-one reading. A little guidance from you on educationally sound techniques to enhance reading or math skills, for example, ensures success for volunteers and the students they help.

Volunteers' Box

Design a Volunteers' Box to hold several different tasks, each accompanied by a set of directions. Through the class newsletter or a special note, tell parents about the box and invite them to visit the classroom and choose a task from the Volunteers' Box. Place the box near the entrance to the classroom so that, without interrupting the flow of class, volunteers may enter your room, grab a project, and get busy. Include both in-school projects and tasks that volunteer parents or grandparents may work on at home.

No man is wise enough by himself.
    – Titus Maccius Plautus, ancient
    Roman Poet

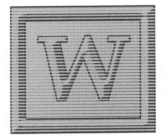

Web Sites with Wisdom

Looking for a word from the wise and your mentor is unavailable? Don't worry. Good advice, tips, and knowledge are merely a URL away. Search these Web sites for what you need, whether it's ideas for lesson plans, techniques for coping with specific behaviors, or strategies from veteran teachers.

Classroom Management

www.kimskorner4teachertalk.com

A language arts teacher's Web site for colleagues in which classroom management is but one topic covered.

www.disciplinehelp.com

This Master Teacher site offers solutions for handling 117 classroom discipline problems.

www.pecentral.org/climate/disciplinelinks.html

A page of links about creating positive learning environments by PE Central, a site for health and physical educators.

http://drwilliampmartin.tripod.com/classm.html

A streamlined collection of classroom management and discipline Web sites originally created by Monmouth University graduate students.

Health and Safety

www.kidsource.com

In-depth education and healthcare information.

www.americanschoolsafety.com

Resources to assist the administration and staff of elementary and secondary schools by providing audit services and developing written protocols for use during emergency situations.

www.cpsv.org

A resource center for efforts that promote safer schools and foster positive youth development.

www.keepschoolssafe.org
> A school safety and security resource.

www.mentalhealth.org/schoolviolence
> A school violence prevention, safety, and security resource with a focus on strengthening healthy child development.

Lesson Plans

www.teachercreated.com
> An educational publishing company of products "created by teachers for teachers and parents."

www.teachers.net
> Teacher resources including lesson plans, distance learning, chatrooms, Web tools, and more.

www.teachervision.fen.com
> Materials to enhance curriculum, to enrich students, and to help teachers make their professional lives a bit easier.

Parents

www.psparents.net
> A resource guide and information source for parents.

Professional Development

www.nbpts.org
> National Board for Professional Teaching Standards

www.ed.gov/pubs/TeachersGuide/index.html
> Teacher's Guide to the U.S. Department of Education.

www.prgaustin.com
> Publishers Resource Group, Inc., a company of educators who are dedicated to student success by creating outstanding curricula, assessments, and instructional tools for the K–12 classroom.

www.edweek.com
> The online *Education Week* newspaper covering current educational topics, issues, and events.

Special Needs Students

http://ericec.org
> The ERIC Clearinghouse for Special Education, Gifted Education, and Related Services.

www.ld.org
> Official site of the National Center for Learning Disabilities.

www.ldonline.org
> Resources for parents and teachers regarding learning disabilities.

www.ed.gov/offices/OSERS/IDEA
> Official site for the Office of Special Education Programs.

www.ncela.gwu.edu
> National Clearinghouse for English Language Acquisition and Language Instructional Programs.

www.nabe.org
> Official site of the National Association for Bilingual Education.

Wellness

Organizing and maintaining your classroom includes being aware of and prepared for the medical needs of your students and possible medical emergencies. Give your room and yourself a wellness checkup:

- **Review student medical-information cards.** It is important to be aware of students' health issues. Know students' allergies to food, insect bites, bee stings, and airborne contaminants. Also be aware of medical conditions, including attention deficient hyperactivity disorder (ADHD), asthma, diabetes, epilepsy, or heart conditions.
- **Create a class medical list.** Ask the school nurse or office personnel for medical information about your students. Using that information, make a list, including the student's name, the nature of the concern, and its required treatment and medication. Be sure to have the medicine's exact name, dosage, and frequency.
- **Share list appropriately.** Place copies of the list in your plan book and substitute-teacher folder, and share the list with your students' other teachers. Let the cafeteria manager know about students' food allergies. Be discriminating when sharing the list, because medical information is confidential and you must safeguard students' privacy.

- **Check the school policy on medication.** Learn the school's procedure for administering medicine at school and while on field trips. Most schools have specific forms for logging the time the medication was administered, the dosage, and the method (e.g., oral), which usually must be submitted to the clinic at the end of the field trip.

- **Learn care procedures.** Knowledge of basic first aid is important, but you also must know what steps to take if one of your students with medical concerns has a severe reaction—as with children who have diabetes, severe allergies, or are prone to seizures. For example, students with severe allergic reactions to bee stings often carry an EpiPen® to counteract a reaction. Learn from the nurse how to administer the device, and whether it should be carried throughout the day.

- **Plan ahead for emergencies.** Learn the school's procedure for a medical emergency, including moving from the classroom or playground to the clinic, and then plan your classroom emergency plan from it. When going to recess, for example, you may decide that it's helpful to carry a clipboard with your class list of medical information, clinic passes, and a pen. Take a first-aid and CPR class.
  – Adapted from "Wellness Check" by Madeline Kovarik, *New Teacher Advocate*, Fall 2004

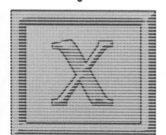

X-pect to Be Tested

Your students will test you, especially in the area of classroom management. They will want to know how far they can push you, whether you are consistent, and if you mean what you say. Why? Because you are a teacher, you are new to them, and well, they're kids! Don't feel like you have to be a drill sergeant to command respect, but do be firm. Above all, be consistent. Don't say something that you can't carry out. Making idle threats has gotten many beginning teachers in a bind. Once students realize threats won't be followed through, they have victory! When you set consequences, choose options you can and will implement.

X-tra Efforts Pay Off

Though your students may not admit it, they typically appreciate the extra efforts you make to help them, connect with them, and show you care. When you see that a student is troubled, it may mean the world to that student for you to say "Is there anything I can do to help?"

Take a few minutes daily to converse casually with your students. Ask the football player how the season is going; listen to the girl eagerly waiting to tell you about the movie she saw over the weekend. Sprinkle compliments around the room; praise is powerful.

Extend X-tra effort to parents. Help them feel welcome in and important to the classroom. Pass along a positive comment about their child. Taking the time to call or e-mail parents good news cultivates an affirming relationship with parents and students. Build a good relationship that will sustain contact about less positive behavior. When students believe you truly care about them, they are much more likely to be respectful.

Y Is a Good Question

"Why do we have to do this?" or "Why do we have to learn about that?" are common *why* questions students ask. Why questions sometimes seem disrespectful, but they need not be. When students understand the purpose of a rule, lesson, or assignment, they relate better to what is being asked of them and are more likely to engage in the activities. If you explain the rationale behind the rule or activity when introducing it, you'll avoid why questions later. For example, when you tell students that gum chewing is not allowed in the classroom, explain that too often ABC gum ends up on the desks, chairs, and carpet.

You Can Do It!

If you are feeling fearful, beware. Students are keenly intuitive. Do everything in your power to mask your fears and appear confident. Don't let them see you sweat, or they will seize the opportunity to walk all over you. Remind yourself that you are the adult and that you are in control,

- even if you don't feel that way. You do have the final say about what
- happens in your classroom.

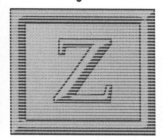

Zingers

Many teachers show their sense of humor through quips they make to students. Unfortunately, these remarks often slip into zingers—sarcastic or critical comments meant to
- be witty, but inappropriate when directed at students. Wit and humor
- that draw smiles or laughter refresh you and the students. Zingers detract
- from your professionalism, perhaps putting you at the students' level,
- and risk offending someone. Stick to professionalism and wit.

Zingers

Are you cruisin' for a bruisin'?
Shut your mouth.
Don't make me come over there!
I'm sick of your face.
Shut up!
Profanity

Most of the trouble and friction among people, in or out of school, is caused by putting others down.

> – William Glasser, Psychiatrist, Counselor, and Lecturer

Z—Last Letter in the Alphabet, Last Word in Classroom Management

Now that you've read classroom management from A–Z, you can enter your classroom as an expert with all the answers, right? Sorry, but that's not the message—or the reality. From A–Z, this book has shown you various techniques for running a classroom that you can apply immediately or transform into a style that works best for you. It also has directed you to other resources for strategies and ideas not included here.

In the end, this book is a tool and a guide, not a magic wand. Becoming an effective classroom manager is a process, a journey. With each group of students, you'll encounter something new. When a lesson doesn't go well or a student gets the best of you, learn from what happened and let it go. Start over the next day and leave the past behind.

Extras

References

Albert, L. 1990. *Cooperative discipline: Classroom management that promotes self-esteem*. Circle Pines, MN: American Guidance Service.

Albert, L. 1996. *Cooperative discipline: Implementation guide*. Circle Pines, MN: American Guidance Service.

Batsche, G. M., and H. M. Knoff. 1994. Bullies and their victims: Understanding a pervasive problem in the schools. *School Psychology Review* 23(2): 165–74.

Center for the Advancement of Mental Health Practices in Schools. 2005. *Portfolio examples*. Columbia: University of Missouri.

Charles, C. M. 2004. *Building classroom discipline,* 8th ed. Boston, MA: Allyn & Bacon.

Craig, D. 2003. Brain-compatible learning: Principles and applications in athletic training. *Journal of Athletic Training* 38(4): 342–49.

Dreikurs, R., P. Cassel, and E. D. Ferguson. 2004. *Discipline without tears: How to reduce conflict and establish cooperation in the classroom,* revised ed. Hoboken, NJ: Wiley.

Erwin, J. C. 2003. Giving students what they need. *Educational Leadership* 61(1): 19–24.

Glasser, W. 1969. *Schools without failure*. New York: Harper & Row.

Glasser, W. 1990. *Choice theory in the classroom*. New York: Harper & Row.

Glasser, W. 1998. *The quality school: Managing students without coercion*. New York: HarperCollins.

Gordon, T. 2003. *Teacher effectiveness training*. New York: Three Rivers Press.

Kovarik, M. 2004. Wellness check. *New Teacher Advocate* 12(1): 7.

Kriete, R. 2003. Start the day with community. *Educational Leadership* 61(1): 68–71.

Marzano, R. J., and J. S. Marzano. 2003. The key to classroom management. *Educational Leadership* 61(1): 6–14.

McLoughlin, A. S. 2003. Just the faqs please. *New Teacher Advocate* 11(1): 10.

Preskill, S. L., and R. S. Jacobvitz. 2001. *Stories of teaching: A foundation for educational renewal*. Upper Saddle River, NJ: Prentice Hall.

Sapon-Shevin, M. 1998. *Because we can change the world: A practical guide to building cooperative, inclusive classroom communities.* Boston: Allyn & Bacon.

Wong, H. K., and R. T. Wong. 2004. *The first days of school: How to be an effective teacher*, book and CD-ROM ed. Sunnyvale, CA: Harry K. Wong Publications.

Resources

Bullying

www.nobully.org.nz/advicek.htm
  Information about and support in dealing with bullying problems for kids, adults, and schools.

www.bullying.co.uk
  Help and advice for parents, kids, youth leaders, and schools. Includes panel discussion, legal advice, tips, sample letters, etc.

www.scre.ac.uk/bully
  Research-based information on bullying in schools and the effectiveness of various approaches to its prevention.

www.education.unisa.edu.au/bullying
  Information to help people understand more about bullying in schools and how it can be stopped.

Discipline

http://challengingbehavior.fmhi.usf.edu/fba.htm
  Center for Evidence-Based Practice: Young Children with Challenging Behavior. 2005. Functional behavioral assessment. Tampa: University of South Florida.

Curwin, R., and A. Mendler. 1999. *Discipline with dignity.* Alexandria, VA: Association for Supervision and Curriculum Development.

Enz, B., S. Kortman, and C. Honaker. 2003. *Ready, set, teach! A winning design for your first year.* Indianapolis, IN: Kappa Delta Pi, International Honor Society in Education.

General

www.kdp.org/teacherresources/teacherresourcehome.php
  This page on the KDP Web site provides links to other sites covering various topics related to teaching and classroom management.

Organization

Bestor, S. M. 1999. *How to organize your classroom.* Westminster, CA: Teacher Created Materials.

Jacobson, J., and D. Raymer. 1999. *The big book of reproducible graphic organizers: 50 great templates to help kids get more out of reading, writing, social studies and more.* Jefferson City, MO: Scholastic.

Schlenger, S., and R. Roesch. 1999. *How to be organized in spite of yourself: Time and space management that works with your personal style.* New York: Signet.

Thompson, J. G. 2002. *First-year teacher's survival kit: Ready-to-use strategies, tools & activities for meeting the challenges of each school day.* San Francisco, CA: Jossey-Bass.

Problem Solving

Gossen, D. C. 1996. *Restitution: Restructuring school discipline.* Chapel Hill, NC: New View Publications.

McAllister, H. C. 2003. 21st century problem solving: A modern approach to reliable problem solving across the curriculum. Available at: *www.hawaii.edu/suremath/home.html.*

Rewards

Cherry, C. 2001. *Please don't sit on kids: Alternatives to punitive discipline,* 2nd ed. Columbus, OH: McGraw-Hill Children's Publishing.

Kohn, A. 1996. *Beyond discipline: From compliance to community.* Alexandria, VA: Association for Supervision and Curriculum Development.

Kohn, A. 1999. *Punished by rewards: The trouble with gold stars, incentive plans, A's, praise, and other bribes.* Boston: Houghton Mifflin.

www.educationworld.com/clsrm_mgmt/index.shtml#rewards. Teacher-tried reward systems

www.theteachersguide.com/ClassManagement.htm. Rewards, classroom management, and discipline

Routines

Guillaume, A. M. 2004. *K–12 classroom teaching: A primer for new professionals,* 2nd ed. Upper Saddle River, NJ: Prentice Hall.

Kriete, R. 2002. *The morning meeting book,* 2nd ed. Turners Falls, MA: Northeast Foundation for Children.

Partin, R. L. 1999. *Classroom teacher's survival guide: Practical strategies, management techniques, and reproducibles for new and experienced teachers.* West Nyack, NY: Center for Applied Research.

Newsletter

Consider the following suggestions when creating your special newsletter.

Contact information

A word from the teacher

Lesson of the week

Homework guidelines

Volunteer acknowledgments and opportunities

Upcoming events

Tips (study or classroom tips and parenting tips)

Reminders (basic school procedures and policies, homework hotline info, your expectations, papers for parents to return)

Fact of the week

Project or classroom supplies needed

Sample Classroom Arrangement #1

| Teacher's Desk | Library Area | Small–Group Work Table |

Carpeted
Work Space

Blackboard

Sink Area

Learning Center

Learning Center

Sample Classroom Arrangement #2

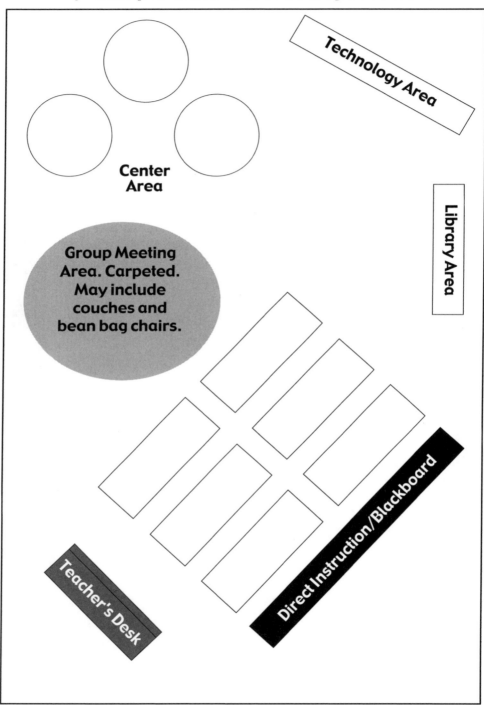

Technology Area

Center Area

Library Area

Group Meeting Area. Carpeted. May include couches and bean bag chairs.

Direct Instruction/Blackboard

Teacher's Desk

Checklists

Room Arrangement Checklist

When planning the physical arrangement of your classroom, take into consideration the various activities that will take place. Think about your plans as well as student movement around the room.

_____ Will your students access learning centers?

_____ Do you want to make room for a comfortable, quiet place to read?

_____ Will technology be available in your classroom?

_____ Taking into account the types of activities you plan, how can you arrange the space to keep noise, disruptions, movement, and distractions at a minimum for you and the students?

_____ Is there easy access to materials, clean-up areas, sinks, outlets, and storage areas?

_____ Does your arrangement allow students to go from one area to another without disturbing others?

_____ What level of interaction would you like among the students? Do you want to cluster students to encourage interaction or incorporate spacing appropriate to independent work time?

_____ What about you? How much work space will you want? Have you designated a personal storage area for yourself?

_____ Will you need a space for a classroom pet?

_____ Do you have a large area for group instruction and class meetings?

_____ Is the overall arrangement comfortable or cluttered?

Environment Checklist

Is your classroom student friendly and conducive to learning? Check it against this list.

_____ The environment conveys a welcoming and comfortable atmosphere.

_____ The environment suggests a sense of safety and security for students at the grade level being taught.

_____ The room boasts a "chill-out corner," a get-away area decorated in soft, calming colors such as blue or green where students can relax.

_____ Stimulating visual displays, manipulatives, and materials fill the room with the purpose of rousing students' curiosity about learning and curriculum content.

_____ The classroom is orderly and organized.

_____ Ample space separates classroom elements, such as desks, learning centers, and group areas, allowing students to move easily around the room.

_____ The classroom provides space for each student to store personal belongings.

Field Trip Checklist

_____ Preliminary visit to field trip site

_____ Site determined/schedule made

_____ Approval from administration

_____ Permission slips distributed with informational letter to parents
(This letter should provide information about the trip's purpose,
schedule, what to bring and wear, as well as transportation
arrangements.)

_____ Transportation arranged

_____ Site reservations made

_____ Tickets/funding obtained

_____ Chaperones identified and trained

_____ Students grouped and matched with chaperones

_____ Permission slips returned

_____ Emergency information list compiled

_____ Materials prepared

_____ Site directions prepared

_____ Student prep completed

Parent-Teacher Conference Preparation Checklist

_____ Send a letter to parents inviting them to identify questions that they would like you to address when they come to meet with you. (This proactive approach allows you to prepare for any special concerns they might have.)

_____ Gather tests, anecdotal records, portfolios, and other work samples to show parents.

_____ Prepare an index card noting key items to cover at the conference. See example on next page.

_____ Arrange seating so that you and the parents are on the same level. A large table works well. If a table is unavailable, you and the parents should sit in the students' desks. Equal seating ensures that you don't come off as being superior to the parents.

_____ Dress and act professionally. Don't drink or smoke prior to the conference.

_____ Greet parents warmly. Be sure you know their proper names, especially in blended family situations.

_____ End the conference with a summary of the discussion and any actions to be taken. Parents should leave with a sense of hope and encouragement for their child.

_____ Document items discussed, particularly when specific actions must be taken.

Parent–Teacher Conference Report

Student's Name_____

Date _____

Strengths	Concerns	Questions

Actions Recommended

_____

_____

_____

_____

_____

_____

_____

_____

_____

_____

_____

_____

_____

_____

_____

_____

Progress Report

Student_____

Grade _____

Teacher(s)_____

Date _____

Subject	Satisfactory Progress	Concerns and Issues Needing Attention	Positive Developments
Reading			
Math			
Science			
Social Studies			
Language Arts			
Art			
Music			
Conduct			
Work Habits			

Family Science Night

Promote family involvement with an event that features an aspect of the curriculum. One successful activity is Family Science Night. Invite students and their parents to the school for an evening of hands-on science activities. While this event takes some careful planning and preparation, it can be a wonderful and enjoyable learning experience for everyone. Let the following steps guide your own amazing Family Science Night.

1. **Set a time and place.** Arrange a suitable date and select a room that can accommodate either several large tables or many smaller ones with space left over for participants to engage in hands-on activities. Obtain permission and support for this event from your building administrator.

2. **Plan the activities.** What activities will make up Family Science Night? They should be engaging, meaningful, and simple enough to be accomplished in a short period of time. If your school is located near a college or university, try to partner with preservice teachers to plan, develop, and possibly carry out the activities. Extra helpers are a must for a successful evening, so if preservice teachers aren't available, seek assistance from upper grade or high school students and colleagues. Approach school clubs for help; they can count it as a service activity.

3. **Obtain materials.** Determine what supplies you'll need, and seek funding or material donations from the school, parent-teacher organization, local businesses, or parents.

4. **Create directions.** Outline easy-to-follow steps for each activity and make enough copies for each activity table. The directions must be clear and concise so that students and parents can perform the experiments with minimal assistance from a teacher.

5. **Prepare invitations.** Create an invitation that includes an RSVP form. Knowing how many people will attend lets you plan accordingly. At this point, you should have determined whether or not other classes are participating in the event. Working with a team of teachers helps share the load of planning and running a curriculum night.

6. Produce an Activity Pack. Provide a list of all the activities available during the Family Science Night, along with directions, supplemental ideas, and resources. Make these packets available for each family. Offering a take-home packet extends the benefit of the event beyond one evening, supplies additional activities, and lets families try experiments they didn't work on during Family Science Night. Having something to show for the evening's efforts is always a plus.

7. Food and beverage. Determine whether or not to have snacks available. Food and drink would be welcome to attendees who didn't have time for dinner, yet it would be more work for you. Your school's parent-teacher organization might consider doing a fund-raiser for the occasion.

8. Participation recognition. Do you want to give certificates of participation or ribbons for attendance? Recognizing participation can help students feel validated. Another way to acknowledge and reward attendance and participation is to have a few Make-and-Take activities that students and parents work on together and take home.

9. Organize. Organize all materials and arrange the room before Family Science Night commences. Enlist the help of a set-up committee. Carefully consider the placement of each activity based on materials to be used. For example, does the activity require access to water or an electric outlet? In addition, you'll want each activity area to look interesting and appealing to encourage engagement.

10. Greet. Recruit volunteers to greet and register participants.

11. Circulate. Throughout the evening, go around the room to answer questions, address problems, and talk with your students and parents.

12. Clean up. It will be a long day, so be sure you've recruited a clean-up crew to help at the end of the evening.

13. Share with the community. Let the local media know about Family Science Night ahead of time in case a reporter or photographer can capture the event. If no one is available, send a brief article and a couple of pictures for the paper's education page. Don't forget to share the success of your event at your school— through morning announcements, newsletter, or another medium. Take part in promoting good news about your school!